fish & seafood
cookbook

Consultant editor
Susanna Tee

Love Food ® is an imprint of Parragon Books Ltd

Parragon
Queen Street House
4 Queen Street
Bath BA1 1HE, UK

ISBN: 978-1-4075-5453-2

Printed in China

Created and produced by The Bridgewater Book Company Ltd
Project editing by Tom Kitch
Internal design by Anna Hunter-Downing
Illustrations by Coral Mula
Photography by Clive Bozzard-Hill
Home economy by Philippa Vanstone

NOTES FOR THE READER

This book uses both metric and imperial measurements. Follow
the same units of measurement throughout; do not mix metric
and imperial. All spoon measurements are level: teaspoons are
assumed to be 5 ml, and tablespoons are assumed to be 15 ml.
Unless otherwise stated, milk is assumed to be semi-skimmed,
eggs and individual vegetables such as potatoes are medium
and pepper is freshly ground black pepper. Sufferers from liver
disease and those with weakened immune systems should never
eat raw fish. Likewise, pregnant women, nursing mothers and
young children should avoid eating fish raw, especially larger
species such as swordfish and tuna, which tend to have high
concentrations of mercury. Recipes using raw or very lightly
cooked eggs should be avoided by infants, the elderly, pregnant
women, convalescents and anyone suffering from an illness. The
times given are an approximate guide only. Preparation times
differ according to the techniques used by different people and
the cooking times may also vary from those given. Optional
ingredients, variations or serving suggestions have not been
included in the calculations.

PICTURE ACKNOWLEDGEMENTS

The Bridgewater Book Company would like to thank Corbis for
permission to reproduce copyright material on pages 2. 10, 12, 16
and on the front cover.

CONTENTS

1 INTRODUCTION

2 FISH NIBBLES

3 FISH FIRST

7 HEARTY MAIN DISHES

8 BARBECUES AND GRIDDLES

1

The Fish and Seafood Cookbook is a comprehensive guide to preparing, cooking and serving every kind of fish and shellfish. Confirmed fish devotees will treasure having all their favourite, classic recipes in one volume, in addition to a range of new, imaginative ideas, while those who may find fish preparation rather daunting will be enlightened, reassured and inspired.

INTRODUCTION

The Fish Directory at the front of the book introduces the fabulous wealth of healthy, delicious food that our waters – both fresh and sea – can offer. All the basic techniques for preparing and cooking these different varieties of fish and shellfish are then explained and demonstrated in detail. The collection of recipes that follows caters for every meal type and occasion, from elegant finger food to hearty main meals, and encompasses all the popular cuisines around the globe, from the Mediterranean to Mexico.

FISH AS FOOD

There are about 21,000 species of fish in the world and, perhaps surprisingly, up to 120 commercial species available to buy as food. Fish and shellfish come in all different shapes, sizes and colours, from the sea, rivers and lakes, from cold waters and warm waters. Fish fits easily into today's lifestyle. It is light, elegant, substantial and nutritious. Cooking fish is also quick and easy, making it a perfect fast food for busy cooks.

Not only does fish come in all shapes and sizes, it also comes whole, filleted, sliced, boned, skinned and canned. The choice appears almost endless and, on top of that, it is available all the year round.

The range of fish and fish dishes can sometimes appear daunting, or even off-putting. However there are excellent reasons to learn more about cooking fish.

Firstly, fish is good for our bodies and souls, from head to toe. It is high in protein, vitamins and minerals, and low in saturated fat. It's the perfect addition to our diet, keeping our hair, skin, eyes, teeth and bones in good health. Research has also shown that eating a diet containing oil-rich fish aids a healthy heart and helps our brains to perform, leading to a longer, healthier life.

FOOD FOR THOUGHT?

Some researchers have claimed that eating oil-rich fish can boost our brain power and decrease the risk of dementia, depression and poor memory. Just one 140 g/5 oz serving or two smaller servings of oily fish will provide a week's supply.

As well as being good for you, fish is good to eat. The huge variety of recipes, from all over the world, pay tribute to the versatility and popularity of fish as the basis for a tasty meal for all the family. In addition, selecting and cooking fish can be as simple or as complicated as you want it to be. But for those who find it difficult to know where to start, help is at hand.

This book will take you through selection, preparation and cooking the most common types of fish and seafood.

Remember, you can also ask your local fishmonger for advice or to prepare the fish for you. This way, you can make sure that your fish will be as fresh and tasty as possible. Fish is the dish of the moment – try it and you will soon be hooked!

SEA OF ROMANCE

While it has long been considered a myth that oysters are an aphrodisiac, it is true that shellfish, and in particular oysters, contain high levels of zinc, a mineral that is important for male fertility and good health.

NUTRITION

Fish is good for you: it's official. It is an excellent source of first-class protein, low in fat in the case of white fish, low in salt, and contains varying degrees of vitamins and minerals, such as vitamins A and D in oil-rich fish, a range of the B vitamins, iron, calcium, copper, magnesium, manganese, phosphorus, potassium, selenium, sodium, iodine, fluorine and zinc.

FISH RICH IN OMEGA-3 FATTY ACIDS

These include red mullet, grey mullet, halibut, herring, kipper, sardine, pilchard, barracuda, mackerel, dolphin fish, eel, swordfish, salmon, trout, scallops and tuna, but only if it is fresh, as the canning process destroys the omega-3.

HEALTH BENEFITS

Even the fat found in oil-rich fish contains high amounts of the essential polyunsaturated fats called omega-3 fatty acids. These are essential to health because they cannot be produced by the human body. Research suggests that these fatty acids reduce cholesterol absorption and help to lower cholesterol levels in the blood, which prevents the arteries from clogging and averts coronary heart diseases. Even people who have had a heart attack are advised to increase their consumption of oil-rich fish to help prevent another heart attack. There is also some evidence that these omega-3 fatty acids help in the prevention of certain cancers, such as breast, prostate and colon cancer, as well as reducing inflammation in people suffering from rheumatoid arthritis and can even improve brain activity. These important fatty acids are found almost exclusively in oil-rich fish.

LOW IN SALT

Surprising, since most fish spend their lives in salt water!

HEART ATTACKS

Current research suggests that eating at least one portion of oil-rich fish per week, as part of a healthy diet, greatly reduces the risk of having a heart attack.

EATING RAW FISH

Fish is usually cooked before eating but, traditionally, sushi is made with both raw and cooked fish. If you make sushi with raw fish, you must realize that there is an element of risk when eating it. Raw fish is more likely to contain bacteria and parasites than cooked fish because it has not been subjected to the correct amount of heat to destroy them. All the recipes in this book can be made with cooked fish, but if you prefer to use raw fish, then be careful to follow the guidelines below:
• People suffering from certain diseases, such as liver disease, and those with weakened immune systems should not eat raw fish or shellfish.
• Only buy really fresh fish, from a reputable supplier or shop that sells 'sushi grade' or 'sashimi grade' fish.

MERCURY LEVELS

Levels of mercury, which is found in water from naturally occurring sources and industrial pollution, tend to be higher in long-lived, larger oil-rich fish, such as mackerel, tuna, swordfish, shark and marlin. For most people, the levels are too low to be of concern. However, pregnant women, nursing mothers and children under 16 should not eat these types of fish, as the levels of mercury in them can be harmful to a baby's and child's development. However, oil-rich fish such as herring, sardine, pilchard, trout and salmon are safe to eat.

TOXINS IN FISH

Although the incidence of toxin poisoning is very rare, some fish from warm waters eat a toxin in their diet and, in turn, are toxic if eaten by another fish. Fish that are particularly vulnerable include the barracuda, sturgeon, moray eel and some snappers and groupers. The toxins build up over time in the liver, so never eat the liver of these fish, and should you suffer from an extreme headache, tingling, irritation or a rash on the skin, weakness or sickness, seek medical help.

CHOOSING AND STORING FISH

Fish and shellfish are best eaten really fresh, which means straight from the water or within two or three days of being caught. Fish, particularly shellfish, is extremely perishable. The solution is to purchase fish from a reputable fish supplier who has a fast turnover of produce, and this could be your local fishmonger, supermarket fish counter or chilling cabinet, delivery van or market. Carry the fish home in a cool bag and, if possible, plan to eat it on the day of purchase. Chilling slows down deterioration and so, due to its short storage time, many fish are cleaned or filleted and either chilled or frozen on-board fishing boats. This helps to keep the fish in prime condition.

WHICH FISH?

Some varieties of fish are available all the year round, while others are not available during, for example, spawning time. When choosing fish, be flexible and take advantage of the variety of fish on sale as many fish are interchangeable in recipes. It is the fish's fat content that is important in helping to select an alternative fish, as it is this that often determines the fish's flavour, texture, colour and cooking method. Remember too that there is a wide variety of frozen fish available.

Freshness

• The eyes should look bright, full and clear, not sunken, cloudy and dry. Herring's eyes should be a red colour.
• The gills under the flaps on both sides of the fish's head should look bright and be pink or red in colour, not grey or dark green and slimy.
• The body should be plump, stiff and firm, and the scales tightly fitting, not limp.
• The skin should be shiny, bright coloured and moist, not faded and dull.
• The flesh should be firm and elastic and should spring back when you press it with your finger, not leave an indentation. The flesh of fillets and steaks should look freshly cut and moist with a firm texture, not dry and discoloured.
• It should smell fresh and slightly of the sea air, not strongly fishy or of ammonia.
• The shells of shellfish should be undamaged and mussels, clams and oysters should close tightly if touched.
• The tails of prawns and shrimps should curl under them.
• Select crabs by weight, not size, as a good crab should be heavy for its size, and shake the crab and reject it if any water comes from inside it.
• Frozen fish should be frozen hard with no sign of partial thawing and should be in packaging that is undamaged.

IT'S A MYTH

The saying that oysters should only be bought when there is an 'r' in the month has no basis in fact as oysters are good all the year round.

STORAGE

Once you've bought your fish and got it home, unwrap it immediately, place it in a dish, then cover and store towards the bottom of the refrigerator. Shellfish should be put in a container, covered with a wet cloth and stored in the refrigerator. If possible, eat on the day of purchase, otherwise eat within 24 hours. Ready-to-eat cooked fish, such as smoked mackerel, prawns and crabs, should be stored on the shelves above raw fish to avoid contamination. Smoked salmon, once the pack is opened, can be stored in the refrigerator for up to one week, but not beyond its use-by date.

If you have to store fresh fish for longer than 24 hours, freezing is the best option. Firmer-fleshed fish tend to freeze better than less firm-fleshed fish, as they retain their texture during the process. Freeze on the day of purchase and thaw overnight in the refrigerator.

HOW LONG TO FREEZE?

From a safety angle, once the fish is in the freezer it can be stored almost for ever as long as the temperature is maintained at -18°C/0°F. However, from a food value, taste, texture and colour angle, white fish is best stored for up to 3 months and oily fish for up to 2 months.

THE FISH DIRECTORY

The following is a guide to all the main species of fish and shellfish that can be eaten, listed by

their common names, although some fish, confusingly, are known by a variety of different names.

The potted profile for each fish details the various forms in which it can be purchased, for

example whole or in fillets, fresh and canned, and the most suitable cooking methods.

Fresh fish are classified into groups according to their features. Flat fish, which vary in size from a small flounder to a large halibut, have a flat bone structure, a dark upper skin and white belly, their eyes face upwards and they swim on their sides. Round fish also vary in size, from a small sardine to a huge pompano, but all have long, slender, rounded bodies, eyes at the side of their head and all swim with their dorsal fin uppermost. Both flat and round fish live their entire lives in the sea, whereas freshwater fish live in rivers and lakes. Exceptions are the salmon and salmon trout, which live in the sea as adults but migrate to fresh water in order to spawn, and the eel, which travels from fresh water to sea water to spawn.

Shellfish are divided into two groups: molluscs and crustaceans. Molluscs have a soft body that is encased inside one or two protective hard outer shells. The exceptions are the cephalopods, which have tentacles protruding from their head. Crustaceans have hard external shells, which are segmented to allow movement.

Fish can be preserved by canning, hot or cold smoking, salting, drying or pickling as detailed in the Fish Directory under the relevant entry for each fish.

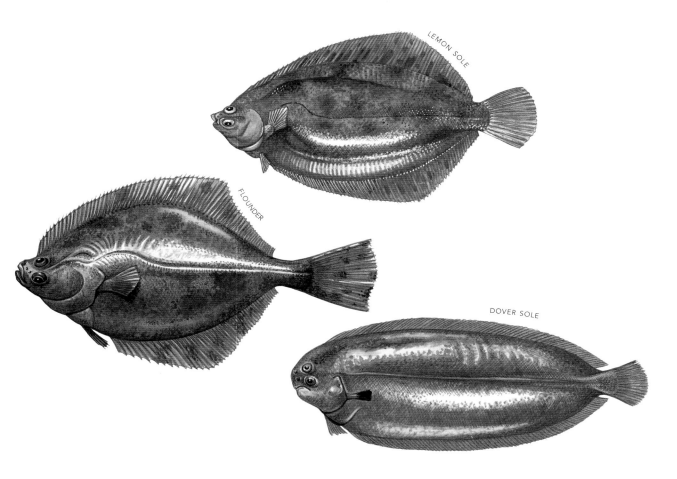

LEMON SOLE

FLOUNDER

DOVER SOLE

FLAT SEAFISH

Plaice
One of the most popular flat fish, it is distinguished by the large red or orange spots on its brown back. It is available whole or in fillets and its white flesh can be fried, grilled, poached, steamed or baked.

Flounder
Flounder is very similar to plaice, but its flavour and texture are not so fine. It is available whole or in fillets and can be cooked in the same way as plaice. In America, flounder is a collective name for several varieties of flat fish.

Brill
Brill is smaller but not dissimilar to turbot in flavour and texture. It is usually sold whole, but can be halved, sliced or filleted and lends itself to being cooked by any method.

Dover Sole
This is one of the finest-flavoured and fine-textured small, flat fish. Its white flesh has an exquisite flavour. Available whole or in fillets, it is traditionally grilled or fried, a classic recipe being Sole Meunière (see page 210).

Lemon Sole
Lemon sole is not dissimilar to Dover sole, although it has much less flavour and its white flesh has a fine texture but is less firm. It can be purchased and cooked in the same way.

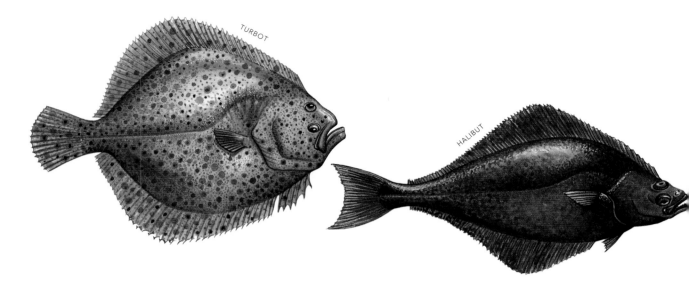

Turbot

This fish, with its huge brown, knobbly body and small head, is considered the finest of the flat fish. It is low in fat, has firm, snow-white flesh and a fine, delicate taste. Depending on its size, it is available whole, in cutlets or in fillets and can be baked, poached or steamed.

Dolphin Fish/Mahi-Mahi/Dorado

Found in warm waters, this is a stunningly attractive fish with a streamlined silver body and black and gold spots, which sadly fade once it is caught. Small fish are sold whole, whereas larger fish are sold in cutlets and fillets. Its flesh is firm and well flavoured, and is very versatile as it can be fried, grilled and cooked in a pie, as in the traditional Maltese pie known as Lampuki.

Halibut

This large flat fish is available whole or as cutlets or fillets. Its flesh is quite oily and its firm texture makes it suitable for baking, braising, poaching or steaming. Halibut is also available smoked.

Dab

This is one of the smallest flat fish and belongs to the plaice family. It has a rough, light brown upper skin and white flesh. It is available whole or in fillets and can be cooked in the same way as plaice.

Skate

This strange-looking fish is shaped like a kite. There are several varieties, of which only the fish's pectoral fin, known as its wings, and small pieces of flesh cut from the bony part of the fish, known as nobs, are eaten. It is low in fat and has a superior flavour. Skate can be fried, grilled, poached or steamed, a classic dish being Skate in Black Butter Sauce (see page 213).

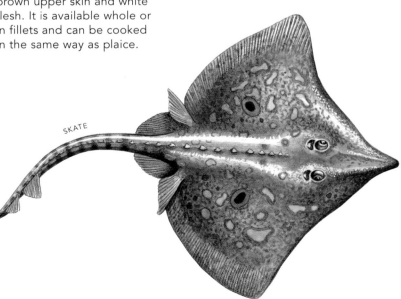

ROUND SEAFISH

Sea Bass/Bass
This large, sleek fish, similar in shape to salmon, has dark, silver-grey scales, which should be removed before cooking, and a white belly. Its firm, white flesh has an excellent flavour. It can be bought whole or in cutlets or fillets and is suitable for poaching or steaming.

Cod
This very popular, white-fleshed fish varies enormously in size and is available whole, which is particularly suitable for baking, poaching or steaming, and in fillets and cutlets, which can be fried or grilled. It is commonly used in cooked dishes such as Fisherman's Pie (see page 216). Much of it is frozen aboard fishing boats. It is also available salted, smoked and dried. Cod's roe is available fresh and smoked and can be used to make Taramasalata (see page 50).

Coley/Saithe/ Coalfish/Pollack
Coley is related to the cod family and has pinkish-grey flesh that becomes white when cooked. Usually available as fillets or cutlets, it can be used in the same way as cod but, as it can be dry, is not suitable for grilling. It is usually used in soups, stews and fish pies.

Haddock
This fish has a firm, white flesh and is closely related to cod, although it is usually smaller and can be distinguished by the dark streak that runs down its back and the two black marks either side of its gills. Sold as fillets or cutlets, it is interchangeable with cod in recipes and is used as an alternative when serving fish and chips. Haddock is often smoked – it is used as such in the well-known dish Kedgeree (see page 136).

SALMON TROUT

HOKI

MONKFISH

SALMON

Hoki

Imported from New Zealand, hoki is related to hake, which in turn is a member of the cod family. Its white flesh is firm, contains very few bones and has a mild flavour. It is sold in fillets or pieces and can be baked, fried or grilled.

Monkfish/ Angler Fish

This deep-sea fish has such a large, ugly head that usually only the tail is sold, boned as a whole piece or skinned and filleted. Its flesh is firm, white and moist, which makes it very suitable for cutting into cubes for kebabs, and can be fried, grilled, baked, roasted, poached or steamed.

Parrot Fish

This beautiful tropical fish with skin ranging in colour from turquoise, green, pink and violet and its round, beak-like face really does look like a parrot. Its flesh is white and firm and is best cooked whole.

Pomfret

This silver, fairly small fish from warm waters is a round fish but, like the John Dory, is laterally compressed and therefore prepared as though a flat fish. It is similar to butterfish, which is popular in America. The flesh is white and delicate and can be stuffed and baked whole or filleted and fried or grilled.

Red Mullet

Red mullet, of which there are several species, is unrelated to grey mullet. It looks attractive, with its crimson skin. It has a firm, white flesh, which has a delicate flavour. Its liver, too, is considered a delicacy, which is why it is usually sold uncleaned. For this reason, it should be eaten fresh before it deteriorates. It must be scaled before cooking and is usually cooked whole, fried, grilled or baked.

Salmon

Most salmon varieties mature at sea and then return to coastal rivers and streams to spawn. Atlantic salmon (wild salmon) and farmed salmon are available, and increased harvests of farmed salmon have made this popular fish more affordable. Salmon has a high fat content and a firm flesh, which can be pink to dark red. It can be poached or baked whole and its cutlets or fillets can be fried or grilled. Its red roe is available as salmon caviar, although this description only really applies to sturgeon roe. It is also popular canned and smoked. Smoked salmon is dry-salted before being smoked and is sold in fillets, which are cut into paper-thin slices.

Salmon Trout/Sea Trout

This fish is often confused with salmon as it also returns from the sea to spawn in coastal rivers. It is smaller than salmon, but larger than trout, has pale pink flesh and can be used in the same way as salmon or trout. However, it is too delicate for smoking. It can be purchased whole or as fillets.

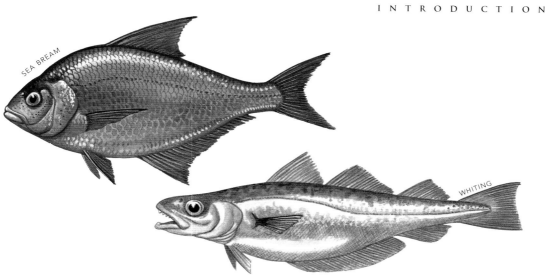

Sea Bream

There are numerous varieties of this large fish, including the red, black, white, pink, ray and gilt-head sea bream. All have firm, white flesh, but the red bream is generally considered to have the best flavour. It is usually cooked whole and can be stuffed and baked, grilled or braised. Their interesting story is that they start life as males and later turn into females!

Whiting

This fish, related to hake, is fairly small and has pale brown skin and a cream belly. Its flesh is white and very soft, with a bland flavour. It can be bought fresh, either whole or in fillets, as well as smoked or salted. It is suitable for frying, grilling, poaching or steaming.

Barracuda

This large, fierce fish from warm waters has white flesh with a firm texture. Small barracuda can be filleted and are suitable for baking, frying, grilling, poaching, steaming and for using in soups and stews. Never eat barracuda raw, or its liver, as it can be toxic (see page 13).

Grey Mullet

This fish, unrelated to the red mullet, looks and tastes similar to sea bass. It has firm, white flesh and can be bought whole or in fillets and is best baked or grilled. Its roe is traditionally used to make Taramasalata (see page 50).

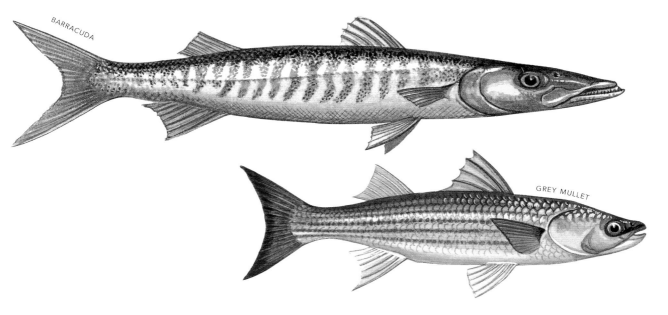

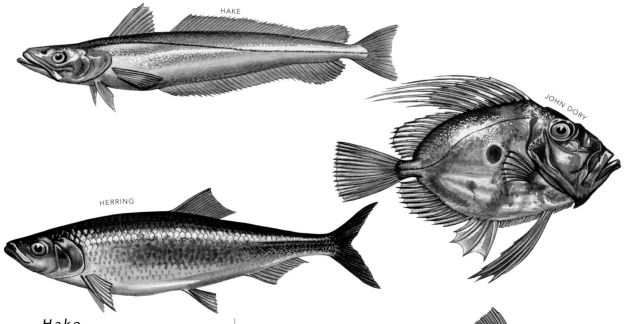

HAKE

JOHN DORY

HERRING

MACKEREL

Hake
This large fish is a member of the cod family, but has a slightly firmer, white flesh. Large hake are cut into fillets or cutlets and these are usually poached, but can also be fried or grilled. Small hake are sold whole. Smoked hake is also available as well as salted hake, which is prepared and used in the same way as salt cod.

Herring
A small, very oily fish, available whole or filleted, that can be fried or grilled or stuffed and baked. Due to its oiliness, the herring is ideal for preserving. Rollmop herrings are raw herrings, boned, rolled up with chopped onions, gherkins and peppercorns and then marinated in spiced vinegar. Herrings are also smoked. Kippers are the most popular form and are sold in fillets or whole, often in pairs. Ideally, dye is not used in the process. Buckling is another version of smoked herring and often considered the best, and there are also bloaters, which are lightly salted, and

smoked herrings. Herrings are also available salted, having been preserved between layers of salt, and they are also sold canned.

John Dory/Dory
In most parts of the world, John Dory is called St Peter or St Pierre (not to be confused with St Peter's Fish), but not in the United Kingdom, Greece or Portugal. Although strictly speaking a round fish, John Dory is laterally compressed and therefore prepared as a flat fish, from which there is little flesh and much waste. It has an ugly head with a very large jaw and a large mark on its side like a thumb print, but it is golden in colour when fresh and its firm,

white flesh has a delicate flavour. It is usually filleted and fried and is a traditional ingredient in Bouillabaisse (see page 121).

Mackerel
This fish, with its striking black markings and silver belly, is particularly oily, which makes it ideal for frying and grilling or stuffing and baking. As its dark flesh has a distinctive flavour, it is often accompanied by a sharp flavoured sauce, such as gooseberry. Mackerel is available whole or in fillets as well as canned or smoked. Smoked mackerel has a rich, strong flavour and is sold in fillets.

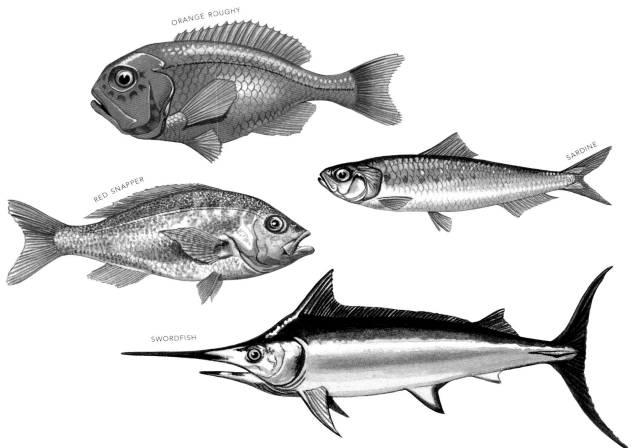

ORANGE ROUGHY

SARDINE

RED SNAPPER

SWORDFISH

Orange Roughy
This fish is bright orange and spiny and, like hoki, is imported from New Zealand. Its flesh is snow white and dense and has a mild flavour. Its unusual feature is that it has a layer of fat beneath its skin, which is removed during filleting. It is interchangeable with cod in recipes.

Pollack
Pollack is closely related to cod, although it is usually smaller and its flavour is not so good. Most is frozen aboard fishing boats. It is cooked in the same way as cod and, with its firm, white flesh, is ideal in mixed fish soups.

Red Snapper
This large fish, identified by its vivid rose-pink skin and red eyes, has white, creamy flesh and is cut into fillets or cutlets, which can be fried, grilled, poached or steamed. Small red snappers are available whole and can be stuffed and baked.

Sardine/Pilchard
These oily, strong-flavoured fish vary in size. The smaller fish are called sardines, whereas the larger, mature fish are known as pilchards, three or four of which make one serving. They are sold fresh and can be fried, grilled or baked. Sardines are also sold canned and can be eaten whole as the preserving process softens their bones.

Swordfish
Swordfish is an enormous fish and is sold as cutlets or chunks. Its firm, dense texture makes it perfect for grilling and frying, although it can also be poached, steamed or baked.

Tuna

There are many species of this large fish, with its dark blue back and silver-grey sides and belly, including the skipjack, yellowfin, bluefin, albacore and big-eye. Its flesh varies in colour from pale pink to dark red and it has a firm, dense texture. It can be bought in chunks or steaks, which can be fried, grilled, braised or poached, but should not be overcooked as it tends to dry out during cooking. Tuna is also sold canned in oil, brine or spring water.

Pompano

This fish from warm waters has a silver skin and fatty flesh. It can be bought whole or in fillets. Its skin should be removed before cooking. It can be baked, fried, grilled, steamed, poached or used in soups and stews.

Conger Eel/ Moray Eel

These are snake-like fish whose bodies can grow up to 2.5 metres/8 feet. The conger eel was once part of the staple diet of the Cornish people, as it was easily caught along the rocky coastline of southern England. It is also available smoked. The moray eel, of which there are several species, are cousins of the conger eel, but much smaller. Both conger and moray eels have firm, white flesh and are usually sold in cutlets. They can be roasted or baked and are good in pies, soups and stews.

Anchovy

These small fish are identified by their large mouths, which almost stretch back to their gills. They are high in fat and, although occasionally available fresh, most are filleted, cured in salt and oil and then canned. They are sold flat or rolled.

Ling

Ling, with its long, brown, eel-like body, is the largest member of the cod family and has soft, white flesh. It is seldom available fresh, but is usually either salted or smoked.

Sprat

Sprat is now rarely sold fresh, but is available smoked. It is very similar to a small herring and can be used in the same way.

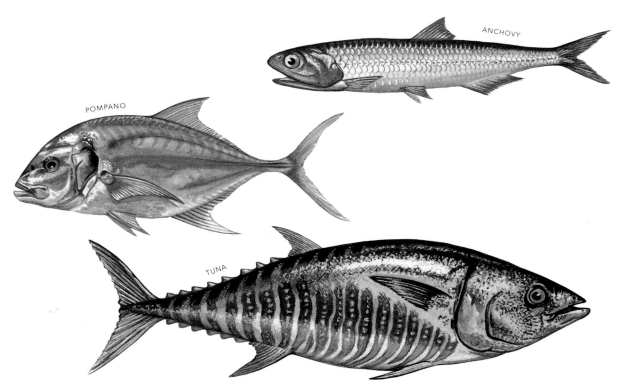

ANCHOVY

POMPANO

TUNA

FRESHWATER FISH

Catfish/Rockfish

There are many species of catfish, many of which are frozen. It is available whole or as fillets and its tough skin must be removed before cooking. It can be fried, grilled, poached, steamed, baked or used in soups or stews.

Trout

There are many varieties of trout, including river, brown, rainbow and salmon trout. It is usually cooked whole and can be baked, fried, grilled, poached or steamed. It is also available smoked, in the same way as smoked salmon.

Char

Char is similar to trout in size and appearance, but more colourful. Its flesh is firm and usually white, or sometimes pale pink. Arctic char is now commonly available, thanks to farming in Iceland and Canada. It is usually sold filleted and as such can be fried, baked or steamed.

Tilapia/ St Peter's Fish

Due to farming, tilapia is now more widely available and can be purchased whole or as fillets. It has a firm texture and is suitable for all cooking methods. An interesting feature of this fish is that the females carry their young in their mouths. They are smaller than the males.

Eel/Common Eel/Elver

This snake-like fish, smaller than the seawater conger eel, lives in rivers and streams and then swims thousands of kilometres to return to the sea and spawn, after which it dies (the opposite migratory habit of salmon). Elvers are baby eels and are no longer eaten, but used to restock fisheries. Killing and skinning a fresh eel is not practical at home and for this reason it is best done by your fish supplier. It can be jellied, fried, grilled, poached, stewed or baked. Eel is also available smoked.

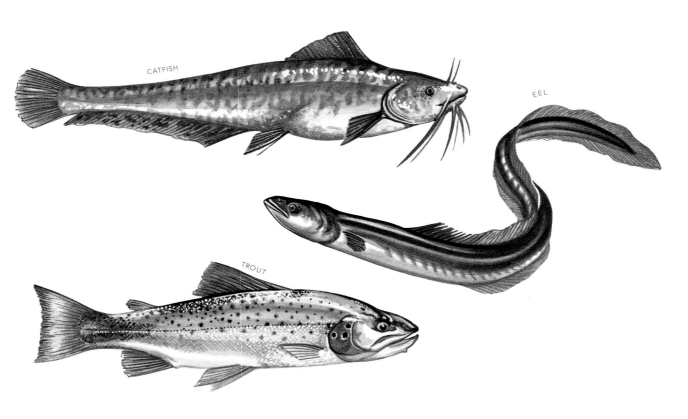

CATFISH

EEL

TROUT

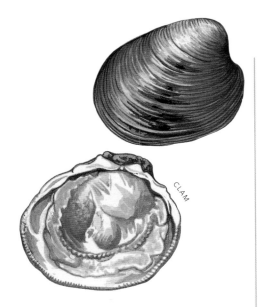

CLAM

SHELLFISH

Clam
There are many varieties of clam, which vary in size and have either soft or hard shells. They are sold live in their shells and larger clams are steamed open, whereas smaller varieties can be eaten raw. They are also sold smoked and canned.

Mussel
Identified by their dark blue shell, mussels cling to rocks or the sea bed and take about two years to reach maturity. They are available live or frozen and are cooked by steaming, which opens their shells. The best known mussels recipe is Moules Marinière (see page 91).

Oyster
There are many varieties of this shellfish, which vary in size. The traditional way of eating them is raw, straight from the half shell with their juices. Shucked (shelled) oysters are available smoked, canned and dried.

Scallop and Queen
Scallops and queens both have ribbed fan shells, but queen scallops, or queenies, are smaller than scallops and are more widely available. Unlike other molluscs, scallops cannot hold their shells tightly closed and die soon after they are taken out of water. This means that they are very perishable and are often removed from their shells and iced aboard fishing boats as soon as they are caught. Both the white muscle and orange coral, or roe, are eaten and have an exquisite, delicate taste. They can be bought fresh or frozen and can be fried, grilled or steamed.

Shrimp
This is the smallest crustacean, of which there are several varieties, such as the brown, pink and deep-water shrimp. Like prawns, they are translucent when alive and turn pink when cooked. Shrimps are mainly sold frozen, but are also available canned, salted and dried.

Prawn
This shellfish is larger than the shrimp and is also available cooked whole or peeled and frozen, canned or dried. A classic way of serving prawns as a starter is Prawn Cocktail (see page 89).

PRAWN

SCALLOP

MUSSEL

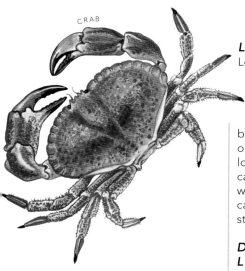

CRAB

Crab

There are several varieties of this crustacean, including the blue or soft-shell crab, the common crab, the green or shore crab and the spider crab. Crab can be bought alive, uncooked in the shell, cooked, with or without the shell, fresh and canned. Its flesh consists of both white meat, found in the claws and legs, and brown meat, found in the body. Crab can be baked, steamed or boiled. Fresh crab can also be purchased 'dressed', with the meat arranged attractively in the shell ready for eating. Canned dressed crab is also available.

Lobster

Lobster, considered by some to be the finest crustacean, can take seven years to reach marketable size. There are several varieties and they can be bought live, when dark blue, or cooked in the shell, when the lobster turns bright pink. Lobster can also be purchased frozen whole or as frozen tails and canned. It can be baked, boiled, steamed or grilled.

Dublin Bay Prawn/ Langoustine/Norway Lobster/Scampi

This attractive shellfish looks like a miniature version of a lobster. It is available live or cooked, with its shell or peeled. When peeled and coated in breadcrumbs, it is known as scampi.

Rock Lobster/ Spiny Lobster

This is another shellfish that looks similar to a small lobster. It is prepared and cooked in the same way as lobster.

Freshwater Crayfish

Also resembling a tiny lobster, these are the only shellfish found in fresh waters.

Octopus

The octopus is a cephalopod and has eight tentacles. It varies in size and large ones – as large as 3 metres/10 feet – are available prepared in pieces and small ones are available whole. Octopus can be poached or used in soups and stews.

Squid

The squid, of which there are several varieties varying in size, is a cephalopod and has ten tentacles. The tentacles are chopped and the body either sliced or kept whole and stuffed. Large squid are usually stewed and small squid can be fried, grilled or poached. Its ink, found in a sac, can also be used in cooking. It is available fresh or frozen.

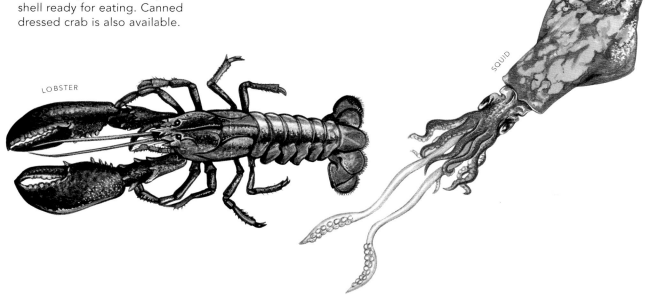

LOBSTER

SQUID

PREPARING FISH AND SHELLFISH

Regardless of the way you intend to cook fish, it must be cleaned first. This means removing the entrails and gills and sometimes the scales and fins. Your fish supplier will often do this for you. If not, use the following guidelines to approach the job step by step.

PREPARING FISH

Trimming round and flat fish

If desired, using kitchen scissors, cut off the gills and fins if the fish is to be served whole. The head and tail may also be cut off using a sharp knife. Rinse the cavity under cold running water. Fins and scales obviously don't need to be removed if the fish is to be filleted or the skin is to be removed after cooking, or in the case of trout, as the scales are part of the skin.

Scaling round fish

This is necessary for fish such as sea bass, salmon and snapper.

Using the back of a knife or a fish scaler, scrape from the tail to the head, away from the direction of the scales, in short, firm strokes to remove the scales. As scales have a tendency to fly everywhere, you might find this a cleaner job if you put the fish in the sink, in a large polythene bag or cover it with a large tea towel. Rinse under cold running water and dry on kitchen paper.

PRESERVING FLAVOUR

Cooking a whole fish with the skin on helps to give the fish flavour and prevent it from drying out during cooking.

Gutting flat fish

The entrails of a flat fish occupy only a small part of the fish's body cavity.

To remove them, open the cavity, which lies in the upper part of the body, under the gills and clean out the entrails as for a round fish.

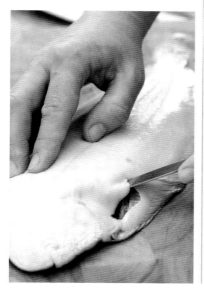

Gutting round fish

1 To remove the entrails, make a slit along the belly from the gills to the tail vent. Pull out the insides and clean away any blood in the cavity.

2 Remove the kidneys by running your thumbnail along the underside of the spine.

3 Rub with a little salt to remove the black skin.

Rinse under cold water and dry with kitchen paper.

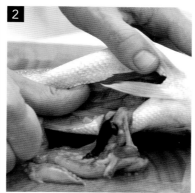

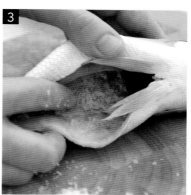

Pocket-gutting round fish

This is suitable for creating a pocket in a fish while keeping the body intact. The fish is gutted through the gills, but it is not as simple a method as gutting a round fish along its belly.

1 Using a sharp knife, cut the end of the gut away from the anus, then open the gill covering and make a slit to reveal the throat.

2 With your fingers, pull out the guts through the throat cavity. Rinse under cold water, removing any remaining innards, and dry on kitchen paper.

Filleting flat fish

Four fillets, two from each side, are usually taken from a flat fish, although sometimes one large fillet is cut from each side and these are known as double or butterfly fillets. To make four fillets, put the fish on a chopping board with its tail towards you. Using a sharp knife, cut around the shape of the head and along the backbone from head to tail. With smooth cutting strokes, working from head to tail, separate the flesh from the bone. Turn the fish over and repeat on the other side.

Filleting large round fish

Two fillets are taken from round fish, although very large round fish, such as John Dory, can be filleted into four, following the flat fish method, or the whole sides can be lifted as described here and then each cut into two fillets.

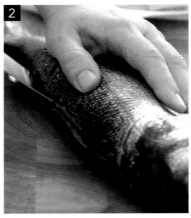

1 Put the fish on its side on a chopping board, with its tail and backbone towards you. Make an angular cut around the gills to the top of the head. It is not necessary to remove either the head or the tail.

2 Cut along the backbone from the head to the tail in order to expose the backbone.

3 With smooth cutting strokes, working from head to tail, separate the flesh from the bones. Turn the flesh over and repeat on the other side, but this time working from tail to head.

Filleting small round fish

This method, also known as butterfly boning, is suitable for small fish such as herrings, mackerel and sardines that are usually cooked whole rather than in fillets.

1 Cut off the head and fins. Make a slit along the belly from the gills to the tail vent and remove the guts. Rinse under cold running water. Put the fish, skin-side up, on a chopping board, and with the heel of your hand, press firmly down on the backbone to loosen it.

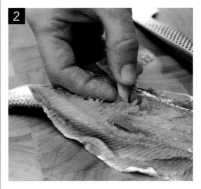

2 Turn the fish over, cut the backbone near the head, then ease the backbone out with your fingers. Remove any pinbones as described in Pinboning Fish (see opposite), then cut off the tail.

Skinning whole round fish

Whole round fish are usually cooked with the skin on, which is then removed before serving.

1 With the point of the knife, loosen the skin under the head. Then, with salted fingers, gently pull the skin down towards the tail, being careful not to break the flesh. Turn the fish over and repeat on the other side.

2 Should you wish to remove the skin before cooking, using a sharp knife, cut along the backbone and across the skin just below the head.

Pinboning fish

Small pinbones are to be found at the top of the flesh of round fish fillets.

To remove them, feel for the bones with your fingertips and then remove them using a pair of tweezers.

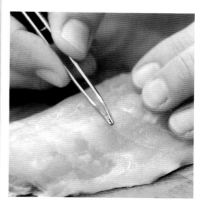

Skinning whole flat fish

Whole flat fish are usually cooked with the skin on. However, Dover and slip soles are traditionally skinned on the dark side only before cooking.

1 Using a sharp knife, make a small cut in the dark skin across the tail.

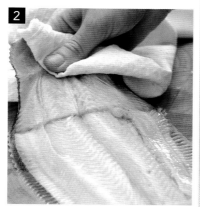

2 Slip your thumb between the skin and flesh of the fish and loosen the skin. Then, holding the tail end firmly with one hand and gripping the skin with a cloth or kitchen paper in the other hand, pull the skin upwards towards the head. A large pinch of salt may help you to grip the flesh.

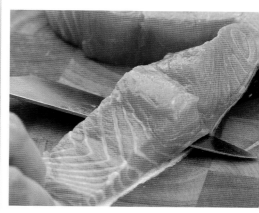

Skinning fish fillets

Put the fish fillet, skin-side down, on a chopping board. Gripping the tail firmly in one hand with a cloth or kitchen paper and with a knife held at an angle, remove the flesh by making a gentle sawing action away from you. A large pinch of salt may help you to grip the tail.

Preparing a fish noisette from a fish cutlet

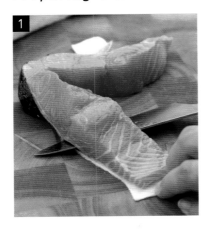

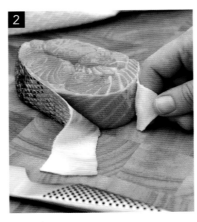

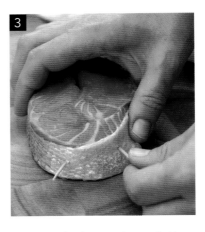

1 After removing the pinbones, using a sharp knife, remove the skin from the flesh halfway around the cutlet.

2 Curl the skinned piece of fish into the centre and wrap the rest of the cutlet around the outside.

3 Wrap the loose piece of skin around the cutlet and secure the whole noisette with wooden cocktail sticks.

Boning a Dover or slip sole

Dover and slip soles can be boned in preparation for stuffing. To do this, skin both sides of the fish as described under Skinning Whole Flat Fish (see page 31).

1 Put the fish on a chopping board with its tail towards you and, using a sharp knife, cut around the shape of the head and along the backbone from head to tail.

2 With smooth cutting strokes, working from head to tail, lift the flesh from the bone, stopping when you reach the fins. Leave the fillet completely attached to the head and tail. Turn the fish around and separate the fillet on the other side of the fish in the same way.

3 Turn the fish over and repeat on the other side, leaving the fillets attached to the fins, head and tail in the same way. Using kitchen scissors, cut away all around the backbone and remove it.

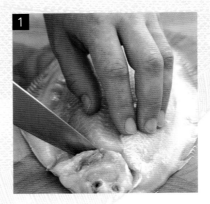

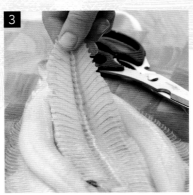

PREPARING CEPHALOPODS

Squid

Put the squid on a chopping board and, grasping the body in one hand, gently pull off the head and tentacles with the other hand. The body entrails will come away at the same time and should be discarded.

1 Cut off the edible tentacles just in front of the eyes and reserve, then squeeze out the small, hard beak and discard.

2 Remove the transparent quill that runs along the length of the body of the squid.

3 Carefully remove one or two of the ink sacs from the head so that you do not pierce them, and reserve them if you want to use the ink in another recipe. Discard the head.

4 Rub off the thin, dark, outer membrane with your fingers. Rinse under cold running water and dry on kitchen paper.

SQUID INK

Squid ink can be used in a black risotto. To use, put the sac in a cup and pierce with the tip of a sharp knife. Dilute the ink with a little water, then pass through a sieve.

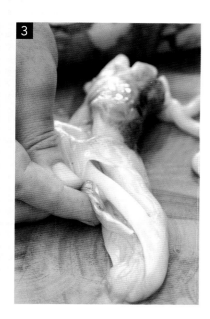

Octopus

Put the octopus on a chopping board and, grasping the body in one hand, firmly pull off the head and tentacles with the other hand. The body entrails will come away at the same time and should be discarded along with the ink sac. Cut off the edible tentacles just in front of the eyes. Rinse the body and tentacles under cold running water and dry on kitchen paper, then beat well with a rolling pin or wooden meat mallet to tenderize the flesh.

PREPARING SHELLFISH

Crab

Crabs are usually sold cooked, but should you buy a live one, the most humane and least traumatic way of killing it is by the following method. Put the live crab in a polythene bag in the freezer for 2 hours to put it to sleep. Bring a large saucepan of heavily salted water to the boil, adding 100 g/3½ oz salt to every 1 litre/1¾ pints. Remove the crab from the freezer, immediately plunge the unconscious crab into the water and cover the saucepan. Return to the boil and simmer for 15 minutes, allowing an extra 10 minutes for each additional crab. Leave to cool in the water.

To prepare a cooked crab, have 2 bowls ready, one for white meat and one for brown meat. Put the crab on its back on a chopping board. Gripping a claw firmly in one hand and as close to the body as possible, twist it off. Remove the other claw and the legs in the same way.

1 Break the claws in half by bending them backwards at the joint. Crack the shells of the claws and larger legs with a rolling pin and remove the white meat with a skewer or teaspoon handle. Reserve the small legs for garnishing.

Put the crab on its back with its eyes and mouth facing away from you.

2 Remove the stomach sac and mouth, which are attached to the back shell, and discard them.

3 Gripping the shell firmly, press the body section upwards and gently pull them apart. Remove the soft grey gills that are attached along the edges of the body and discard.

4 Cut the body into two or four pieces and carefully pick out the flesh. Scoop out the brown meat from the shell.

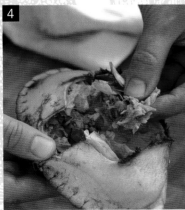

Lobster

A live lobster should be cooked in the same way as a crab (see opposite), but when you remove it from the freezer, weigh it quickly before plunging it into the water. Calculate the cooking time by allowing 18 minutes for the first 500 g/1 lb 2 oz and an extra 11 minutes for every additional 500 g/1 lb 2 oz.

1 To prepare a cooked lobster, put it on a chopping board and twist off the claws and pincers. Crack open the large claws and remove the flesh from them, discarding the membrane. The small claws can be reserved for garnishing.

2 Using the point of a sharp knife, split the shell of the lobster in half from head to tail.

3 Remove the flesh from the tail, reserving the coral (only found in females and at certain times of the year) and, using a skewer, scrape out the flesh from the back legs.

4 Remove and discard from the lobster the thread-like intestine, the stomach sac and the spongy gills.

DON'T SOAK OR FEED SHELLFISH

Never soak shellfish, particularly filter feeders such as oysters, mussels and clams, in cold water as this will kill them. They should also not be fed, for example with oatmeal, while storing them in the refrigerator, as they will perish before cooking.

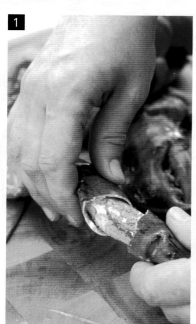

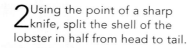
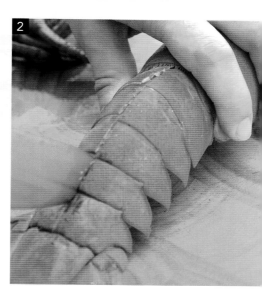
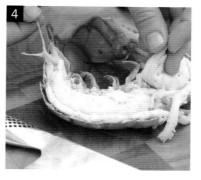

Prawn

1 To peel a prawn, hold its head between your thumb and forefinger and, using the fingers of your other hand, hold the tail and gently pinch and pull off the tail shell.

2 Holding the body, pull off the head, body shell and claws.

3 To devein a prawn, using the point of a sharp knife or skewer, carefully pull out the dark vein that runs down the prawn's back and discard.

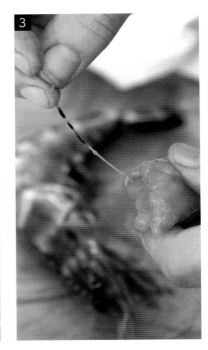

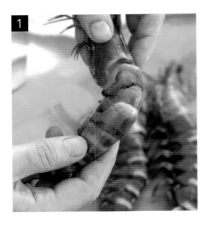

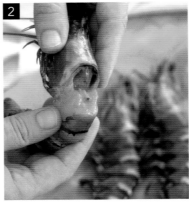

Oyster

Scrub each oyster shell with a stiff scrubbing brush under cold running water to clean. To open an oyster (known as to shuck an oyster), put it on a chopping board, with the rounded side down, and cover with a clean tea towel to protect your hands.

1 Holding the oyster in the cloth and using a strong, short knife or, ideally, a shucking knife, insert the knife at the hinge and prise the shell upwards to open the oyster shell. Take great care when doing this.

2 Slide the knife along the inside of the upper shell to cut the muscle and release the oyster. Try to reserve as much of the juice as possible. Oysters served raw 'on the half shell' are served with their juices in the bottom shell.

Clam

Scrub each clam with a stiff scrubbing brush under cold running water to clean the shell, then put on a chopping board or hold each clam in a cloth in the palm of your hand and prise the shell open at the hinge with a knife, ideally a clam knife.

If the clams are very difficult to open, they can be helped by putting them on a baking tray in a very hot oven for 4–5 minutes until they begin to open.

Loosen the clams and leave each in one half of the shell if you are intending to serve them raw. Reserve any juice from the clams, as this can be strained and used in a sauce. It should certainly not be discarded.

Mussel

Clean each mussel by scrubbing or scraping the shell under cold running water to remove any barnacles, mud or seaweed.

Pull away any beards that are attached to the mussel shells. It is the the beard that the mussel uses to cling to the rocks so you will need to tug hard. If the mussel is open and will not close when tapped sharply with the back of a knife, it is dead and should be discarded.

Also discard any with broken shells or any that feel particularly heavy, as these are probably filled with sand. Put the mussels in a colander and rinse well under cold running water, then drain well.

Scallop

1 Scrub each scallop shell with a stiff scrubbing brush under cold running water to remove as much sand as possible.

2 Discard any scallops that are open and will not close when tapped sharply with the back of a knife. Using a strong knife, prise the shell open. If the scallops are very difficult to open, they can be helped by putting them on a baking tray, with their rounded side uppermost, in a very hot oven for 4–5 minutes until the shells begin to open.

3 Remove and discard the grey beard that surrounds each scallop and the black thread and stomach bag. Detach the scallop and coral from the shell with a spoon. Rinse under cold running water and dry on kitchen paper.

COOKING FISH AND SHELLFISH

Fish lends itself to most cooking methods, as described over the following pages, and the methods can be applied in the same way regardless of the fish. When fish is cooked, it should look opaque, right through to the bone, and the flakes of the fish should be more obvious. Try to avoid overcooking, as it will make the fish shrink, toughen and become dry.

DEEP-FRYING

Small whole fish and small pieces of fish and shellfish, coated in a barrier such as flour, batter or egg and breadcrumbs, are suitable for this cooking method. It is this protective coating that keeps the fish moist, gives it crispness and seals in the flavour. Here are a few rules:

• Use a deep-fat fryer, a heavy-based saucepan or a wok large enough so that the fish is completely immersed in the oil.

• Don't fill the pan more than half full.

• Use a vegetable oil, such as sunflower or corn oil, but not olive oil as it spits.

• The temperature of the oil should be between 180–190°C/350–375°F so that the coating is sealed immediately, which protects the fish from the hot fat and prevents the fat from soaking in and the food becoming greasy. A simple way to test to see if the temperature is correct is to drop a cube of bread in the oil. If it rises to the surface, fizzes immediately and turns brown in 30 seconds, the oil is hot enough.

• Cook the fish in batches so that the pan is not overcrowded and the temperature of the oil doesn't drop. This will assure that the fish is thoroughly cooked, evenly browned and crisp.

• Oil that has been used for deep-frying can be used two or three times before being discarded.

KEEP IT WHITE

Lemon juice, white wine or vinegar, added to the liquid when poaching or steaming fish, helps to keep the flesh of the fish white and firm.

SHALLOW-FRYING

This is suitable for whole fish, steaks, cutlets, fillets and shellfish, which are sometimes coated in flour before frying to protect their flesh, making them crispy and sealing in the flavour. Use a large, uncovered frying pan so that the fish will fit comfortably in it as, if it is over-packed, the temperature of the fat will drop. It is important to use the minimum amount of fat and to keep it hot so that the fish browns without absorbing the fat and becoming greasy. The fat used can be a vegetable oil, such as sunflower oil, clarified butter or butter, which gives a good flavour. If you are solely using butter, heat until it is foaming, but watch it carefully as it burns quickly. Adding a little oil to it helps, as the oil reaches a high temperature before the butter burns.

Don't turn or move the fish too often, as it will stick to the base of the pan. Allow it to brown first before turning. If cooking thick pieces of fish, fry quickly until browned, then reduce the heat and cook until the flesh is tender.

STIR-FRYING

This is suitable for small pieces of firm-textured fish that need only the quickest of cooking. A wok is traditionally used, as its sloping sides make it perfect for continually stirring and tossing the fish. However, a large frying pan can be used as a substitute. Only a small amount of oil is needed and this should be heated until very hot before adding the fish.

POACHING

This is a moist method of cooking most fish, immersed in a liquid, on the hob or in the oven. A fish kettle or large saucepan is used on the hob or a large roasting tin, covered with foil, in the oven. The poaching liquid can be Court Bouillon (see page 44), Fish Stock (see page 44), wine, cider, beer, milk or flavoured water, and sometimes this liquid is then made into a sauce to serve with the fish. It is important that the liquid never boils but just trembles, so that the fish doesn't fall apart. To poach fish, first weigh the fish. Heat the liquid in the saucepan, add the fish, cover and simmer very gently, allowing 10–15 minutes per 450 g/1 lb, according to the thickness of the fish, or about 20 minutes for a small piece of fish.

STEAMING

This is a gentle, moist method of cooking whole fish, fillets, steaks, cutlets and shellfish in a water vapour over boiling water. A steamer, with a tight-fitting lid to trap the steam, is needed but if not available, you can improvise by cooking the fish between two greased plates over a saucepan of boiling water. You could even use a saucepan with a tight-fitting lid and a sieve. The fish should be well seasoned otherwise it may taste bland. The water in the saucepan should be boiling, but watch that it does not bubble up over the fish during cooking.

SEARING AND GRIDDLING

Searing and griddling are suitable for cooking whole and thicker pieces of fish and produce browned skin and flesh. The methods are the same except that seared fish is cooked in a heavy-based frying pan and griddled fish is cooked on a cast-iron, ridged griddle pan or flat griddle plate. The griddle pan or griddle plate is first wiped with just a little vegetable oil, heated until it is very, very hot and the fish, which should also be brushed with a little oil, is placed on it and cooked on both sides until browned.

GRILLING AND BARBECUING

Whole fish, steaks, cutlets, fillets and skewered pieces of fish all lend themselves to these dry cooking methods, but for good results, their thickness should be no more than 5 cm/2 inches and whole fish should be scored at the thickest part of the flesh so that the heat penetrates and cooks the fish right through. Oily fish are particularly suitable, as the natural oils baste the flesh during cooking. Grilled and barbecued fish also benefit from being marinated before cooking and the marinade should be basted over the fish while it is cooking to keep it moist.

It is very important to preheat the grill at its highest temperature before cooking, as intense heat, and being cooked as close to the heat source as possible, is the secret of successful grilled fish. This will cook the fish so that it is browned and crisp on the outside and moist inside. Barbecues should also be preheated and the flames and smoke allowed to die down so that the fish is only cooked over the red hot embers. Brush the grill rack or foil, if using to line the rack, barbecue rack or a fish barbecue holder, and also the fish, with vegetable oil to prevent the fish from sticking. As barbecuing is a method of cooking by intense heat, the fish can dry out quickly, so you may prefer to wrap it in oiled foil, which will help to keep it moist.

BAKING

Baking is an ideal method of cooking whole fish, particularly stuffed fish, as well as steaks and fillets. As this is a method of cooking by dry heat, a knob of butter and a little stock, milk, lemon juice or wine is added to the fish and the fish should be covered to prevent it from drying. This can be done either by covering the dish with foil or by wrapping the entire fish in greaseproof paper, known as en papillote (see the recipe for John Dory en Papillote on page 208). When cooked en papillote, the fish is served in its paper bag.

BRAISING

This is a moist, one-pot method of cooking, usually a whole fish, on the hob or in the oven. The fish is placed on a bed of vegetables with just enough liquid to cover the vegetables, and the pan or dish should always be covered. The fish is then cooked gently. At the end of cooking, the vegetables are discarded and the liquid is usually used to make a sauce to serve with the fish.

STEWING

Whole fish, chunks of fish and shellfish can be cooked in liquid with other ingredients, such as vegetables and flavourings, to form a stew. The fish flavours the liquid but, unlike a meat stew where it is cooked for a long time, the fish in a fish stew is often added to the liquid towards the end of cooking so that it is not overcooked.

Classic fish stews include Bouillabaisse (see page 121), which is traditionally served as two courses, Bourride, where the fish is not left whole as in Bouillabaisse, Matelote, made with fresh water fish, and Cioppino (see page 122) made from shellfish.

MICROWAVING

Microwave ovens are excellent for cooking fish because, as the fish cooks in its own juices, it is a moist form of cooking. However, a few rules should be observed for successful results.
• Arrange the thickest part of the fish towards the edge of the dish.
• Tuck in the tail end of fillets to create a more even shape.
• Don't over-season fish as this causes a rapid loss of moisture.
• Cut pieces of fish into the same size and thickness so that they cook evenly.
• Slash the skin of whole fish in two or three places to allow steam to escape and prevent it from spitting during cooking.
• Cover fish during cooking, unless the recipe says otherwise, to retain the moisture.
• Don't fry fish in the microwave.

DON'T FIDDLE

When searing, griddling, grilling and barbecuing, don't be tempted to turn or move the fish around while cooking, as it may stick to the pan, griddle or rack and fall apart. Ideally, turn the fish only once during cooking.

PREPARING SUSHI

Sushi originated centuries ago as a way of extending the shelf life of dried fish by placing it between layers of vinegared rice. The word sushi refers to the vinegared rice, but the term has been extended to describe a finger-sized piece of raw fish or seafood on a bed of cold vinegared rice.

EQUIPMENT NEEDED

Very little specialized equipment is required, although you can buy sushi-making kits in various outlets, including larger supermarkets. The key to the technique is a bamboo sushi mat with which to make the most common form, rolled sushi. A kit may include a special mixing tub, a pressing box and a spatula.

WHICH FISH?

Meatier types of round fish, such as cod, tuna, salmon, trout, mackerel and eel, are all suitable for sushi, as are prawns, lobster, squid, scallops, crab and fish roe. Smoked versions of haddock, salmon, trout and mackerel are also popular. Many sushi recipes use raw fish. Always buy it from a reliable supplier who offers 'sushi' or 'sashimi grade' fish, which is as fresh as possible, because raw fish contains more bacteria and parasites than cooked fish. Similarly, look for shellfish that come from certified waters. Only buy fish or shellfish on the day you intend to eat it and keep it refrigerated.

PREPARING SUSHI RICE

Sushi is a short-grained rice, and several brands are available. The hot, cooked rice is tipped into a large, shallow dish and sushi rice seasoning spread over the surface. With one hand you mix in the seasoning with a spatula; with the other you fan the rice to cool it quickly. The finished rice should have a shiny appearance and be at room temperature.

PRESENTING SUSHI

Presentation is all, and the best sushi are minor works of culinary art. You need all the ingredients assembled, the rice cooled and garnishes, pickles or dipping sauces prepared so that you can serve the sushi immediately.

Scattered sushi

This is where sushi rice is mixed loosely with other ingredients, and is very easy to make. It is often served as an attractive, individual bowl for each person.

Rolled sushi

These are best made using a sushi mat.

A sheet of nori (dried seaweed), is placed on the bamboo mat and the filling heaped along the bottom third of the nori.

By folding the mat over the filling, then lifting the mat and keeping an even pressure along the length, the roll is formed.

It is cut using a very sharp, wet knife into rounds, which are then turned on one end to present the filling.

Boat sushi

These dishes are prepared by wrapping nori around rice moulded into oval shapes. Using nori is an ideal way to serve sushi with fish roe or soft toppings that would otherwise be messy to handle.

Pressed sushi

This type is made by pressing the rice into a special three-piece bamboo box, although you can improvise using a loose-based tin or terrine tin with drop-down sides. If you have a fixed-base tin, the sushi has to be made upside down, and the sushi turned out, after the flavours have had time to mix and develop.

BASIC RECIPES

The recipes in this book provide an unlimited variety of delicious fish meals. Some of the recipes use a common basic recipe which are referred to on these pages, or you can use these basic recipes as an addition to a dish of your choice.

FISH STOCK

MAKES ABOUT 1.4 LITRES/2½ PINTS

900 g–1.3 kg/2–3 lb fish heads, bones and tails, with any
   large bones cracked and without any gills
1.2 litres/2 pints water
500 ml/18 fl oz dry white wine
1 onion, thinly sliced
1 leek, halved, rinsed and chopped
1 carrot, peeled and sliced
6 fresh flat-leaf parsley sprigs
1 bay leaf
4 black peppercorns, lightly crushed

Put the fish trimmings, water and wine in a large, heavy-based saucepan over a medium-high heat and slowly bring to the boil, skimming the surface constantly to remove the grey foam.

When the foam stops forming, reduce the heat to low, add the remaining ingredients and leave the stock to simmer for 30 minutes, skimming the surface occasionally if necessary.

Strain the stock and discard the flavouring ingredients. The stock is now ready to use or can be left to cool completely, then chilled for 1 day, as long as it is brought to a full rolling boil before use. Alternatively, it can be frozen for up to 6 months.

COURT BOUILLON

MAKES ABOUT 0.6 LITRES/1 PINT

850 ml/1½ pints cold water
850 ml/1½ pints dry white wine
3 tbsp white wine vinegar
2 large carrots, roughly chopped
1 onion, roughly chopped
2 celery sticks, roughly chopped
2 leeks, roughly chopped
2 garlic cloves, roughly chopped
2 fresh bay leaves
4 fresh parsley sprigs
6 black peppercorns
1 tsp salt

Put all the ingredients into a large saucepan and slowly bring to the boil. Cover and simmer gently for 30 minutes.

Strain the liquid through a fine sieve into a clean pan. Bring to the boil again and simmer fast, uncovered for 15–20 minutes, until reduced to 600 ml/1 pint.

Simmer the fish in the court bouillon, according to the length of time required to cook. Drain the fish.

BÉCHAMEL SAUCE

300 ml/10 fl oz pint
  milk
4 cloves
1 bay leaf
pinch of freshly grated nutmeg
25 g/1 oz butter or margarine
2 tbsp plain flour
salt and pepper

Put the milk in a saucepan and add the cloves, bay leaf and nutmeg. Gradually bring to the boil. Remove from the heat and leave for 15 minutes.

Melt the butter in another saucepan and stir in the flour to make a roux. Cook gently, stirring, for 1 minute. Remove the pan from the heat.

Strain the milk and gradually blend into the roux. Return the pan to the heat and gently bring to the boil, stirring, until the sauce thickens. Season to taste.

VARIATIONS

All sorts of ingredients can be added to the basic Béchamel recipe to make interesting sauces which go particularly well with vegetables and fish.

Watercress Sauce
Add 1 small bunch of watercress, finely chopped, to the basic sauce.

Parsley Sauce
Add 2 tablespoons finely chopped fresh parsley to the basic sauce.

Mushroom Sauce
Wash and finely slice 115 g/4 oz button mushrooms, and add them to the basic sauce with 1 tablespoon of finely chopped fresh tarragon.

Lemon Sauce
Add some finely grated lemon rind and juice to the basic sauce.

Mustard Sauce
Add 1 tablespoon French mustard and a squeeze of lemon juice to the basic sauce.

HOLLANDAISE SAUCE

2 tbsp white wine vinegar
2 tbsp water
6 black peppercorns
3 egg yolks
250 g/9 oz unsalted butter
2 tsp lemon juice
salt and pepper

Put the wine vinegar and water into a small saucepan with the peppercorns, bring to the boil, then reduce the heat and simmer until it is reduced to 1 tablespoon (take care, this happens very quickly). Strain.

Mix the egg yolks in a blender or food processor and add the strained vinegar while the machine is running.

Melt the butter in a small saucepan and heat until it turns almost brown. Again, while the blender is running, add three-quarters of the butter, the lemon juice, then the remaining butter and season well with salt and pepper.

Turn the sauce into a serving bowl or keep warm for up to 1 hour in a bowl over a pan of warm water. If serving cold, allow to cool and store in the refrigerator for up to 2 days.

MAYONNAISE

2 egg yolks
pinch of salt, plus extra for seasoning
150 ml/5 fl oz sunflower oil
150 ml/5 fl oz olive oil
1 tbsp white wine vinegar
2 tsp Dijon mustard
pepper

Beat the egg yolks with a pinch of salt. Combine the oils in a jug. Gradually add one quarter of the oil mixture to the beaten egg, a drop at a time, beating constantly with a whisk or electric mixer.

Beat in the vinegar, then continue adding the oils in a steady stream, beating constantly.

Stir in the mustard and season to taste with salt and pepper.

AIOLI

1 large egg yolk
1 tbsp white wine vinegar or lemon juice
2 large garlic cloves, peeled
salt and pepper
5 tbsp extra virgin olive oil
5 tbsp sunflower oil

Put the egg yolk, vinegar, garlic, and salt and pepper to taste in a bowl and whisk until all the ingredients are well blended.

Add the olive oil, then the sunflower oil, drop by drop at first, and then, when it begins to thicken, in a slow, steady stream until the sauce is thick and smooth.

GREEK GARLIC SAUCE

115 g/4 oz whole blanched almonds
3 tbsp fresh white breadcrumbs
2 large garlic cloves, crushed
2 tsp lemon juice
salt and pepper
150 ml/5 fl oz extra virgin olive oil
4 tbsp hot water

Put the almonds in a food processor and blend until finely ground. Add the breadcrumbs, garlic, lemon juice and salt and pepper and mix well together.

With the machine running, very slowly pour in the oil to form a smooth, thick mixture. When all the oil has been added, blend in the water.

Turn the mixture into a bowl and chill in the refrigerator for at least two hours before serving.

TARTARE SAUCE

2 large egg yolks
2 tsp Dijon mustard
$3/4$ tsp salt, or to taste
white pepper
2 tbsp lemon juice or white
  wine vinegar
about 300 ml/10 fl oz sunflower oil
10 cornichons, finely chopped
1 tbsp capers, finely chopped
1 tbsp flat-leaf parsley, finely chopped

Whiz the egg yolks with the Dijon mustard, salt and white pepper to taste in a food processor, blender or by hand. Add the lemon juice and whiz again.

With the motor still running or still beating, add the oil, drop by drop at first. When the sauce begins to thicken, the oil can then be added in a slow, steady stream.

Stir in the cornichons, capers and parsley. Taste and adjust the seasoning with extra salt, pepper and lemon juice if necessary. If the sauce seems too thick, slowly add 1 tablespoon of hot water, single cream or lemon juice.

Use at once or store in an airtight container in the refrigerator for up to 1 week.

SUSHI RICE

250 g/9 oz sushi rice
325 ml/11$^{1}/_{2}$ fl oz water
1 piece of kombu
2 tbsp sushi rice seasoning

Wash the sushi rice under cold running water until the water running through it is clear, then drain the rice. Put the rice in a saucepan with the water and the kombu, then cover and bring to the boil as quickly as you can.

Remove the kombu, then turn the heat down and simmer for 10 minutes. Turn off the heat and leave the rice to stand for 15 minutes. Do not at any point take the lid off the saucepan once you have removed the kombu.

Put the hot rice in a large, very shallow bowl and pour the sushi rice seasoning evenly over the surface of the rice. Use one hand to mix the seasoning carefully into the rice with quick cutting strokes using a spatula, and the other to fan the sushi rice in order to cool it quickly.

The sushi rice should look shiny and be at room temperature when you are ready to use it.

BEURRE BLANC

3 tbsp very finely chopped shallots
2 bay leaves
6 black peppercorns, lightly crushed
3 tbsp white wine, such as Muscadet
3 tbsp white wine vinegar
1$^{1}/_{2}$ tbsp double cream
175 g/6 oz unsalted butter, cut into small pieces
2 tsp chopped fresh tarragon
salt and pepper

Put the shallots, bay leaves, peppercorns, wine and vinegar in a small saucepan over a medium–high heat and boil until reduced to about 1 tablespoon. Strain the mixture through a non-metallic sieve, then return the liquid to the saucepan.

Stir the cream into the liquid and bring to the boil, then reduce the heat to low. Whisk in the butter, piece by piece, not adding the next until the previous one is melted. Whisking constantly and lifting the pan off the heat occasionally will help prevent the sauce from separating. Stir in the tarragon and salt and pepper to taste.

2

Fish and shellfish make ideal finger food – tantalizing, luxurious, melt-in-the-mouth morsels that have instant eye and taste-bud appeal. Whether you are catering for an informal get-together or for special-occasion entertaining, these recipes for both hot and cold nibbles are easy to prepare yet impressive in effect.

FISH NIBBLES

Home-made sushi will certainly provide the wow factor, and here are some stylish blocks, bars and rolls that can all be prepared in advance. Prawns come perfectly proportioned for popping in the mouth, so we have them sizzling in aromatic oil or wrapped in ham. But who can resist a crisp, pastry package hot from the oven? The choice is yours, from crab-filled wontons and filo parcels to tuna boreks.

serves 6 | *prep* 15 minutes, plus 1 hour's chilling | *cook* no cooking required

TARAMASALATA

225 g/8 oz smoked cod roe or fresh
  grey mullet roe
1 small onion, quartered
55 g/2 oz fresh white breadcrumbs
1 large garlic clove, crushed
grated rind and juice of 1 large lemon
150 ml/5 fl oz extra virgin olive oil
6 tbsp hot water
pepper
crackers, potato crisps or pitta bread,
  to serve

TO GARNISH
stoned black Greek olives, sliced
capers, rinsed

Remove the skin from the roe. Put the onion in a food processor and process to chop finely. Add the roe in small pieces and process until smooth. Add the breadcrumbs, garlic and lemon rind and juice and mix well together.

With the motor running, very slowly pour in the oil through the feed tube, then blend in the water. Season to taste with pepper.

Turn the mixture into a serving bowl, then cover and chill in the refrigerator for at least 1 hour before serving. Serve garnished with olives and capers and accompany with crackers, crisps or pitta bread.

makes 18 | *prep* 30 minutes | *cook* 15–30 minutes

TUNA & TOMATO BOREKS

about 18 sheets filo pastry,
   38 x 15 cm/15 x 6 inches each,
   thawed if frozen
vegetable oil, for sealing and
   shallow-frying
sea salt, to garnish
lemon wedges, to serve

FILLING
2 hard-boiled eggs, shelled and
   finely chopped
200 g/7 oz canned tuna in brine,
   drained
1 tbsp chopped fresh dill
1 tomato, peeled, deseeded and very
   finely chopped
1/4 tsp cayenne pepper
salt and pepper

To make the filling, put the eggs in a bowl with the tuna and dill and mash the mixture until blended.

Stir in the tomato, taking care not to break it up too much. Season with the cayenne pepper and salt and pepper to taste. Set aside.

Lay a sheet of filo pastry out on a work surface with a short side nearest to you, keeping the remaining sheets covered with a damp tea towel. Arrange about 1 tablespoon of the filling in a line along the short side, about 1 cm/ 1/2 inch in from the end and 2.5 cm/ 1 inch in from both long sides.

Make one tight roll to enclose the filling, then fold in both long sides for the length of the filo. Continue rolling up to the end. Use a little vegetable oil to seal the end. Repeat to make 17 more rolls, or until all the filling has been used up.

Heat 2.5 cm/1 inch of oil in a frying pan to 180–190°C/350–375°F, or until a cube of bread browns in 30 seconds. Fry 2–3 boreks at a time for 2–3 minutes until golden brown. Remove with a slotted spoon and drain well on kitchen paper. Sprinkle with sea salt. Serve hot or at room temperature with lemon wedges for squeezing over.

makes 12 | *prep* 30 minutes | *cook* 4–6 minutes

TUNA SESAME BLOCKS

8 x 6-cm/3¹/₄ x 2¹/₂-inch piece
  centre-cut tuna fillet,
  2 cm/³/₄ inch thick
2 tsp sesame oil
2 tbsp toasted sesame seeds
3 small sheets nori, cut lengthways
  into 4 strips
2 tbsp vegetable oil

Cut the tuna into 12 cubes. Put the sesame oil in a shallow bowl or on a plate and the sesame seeds in a separate bowl or on a plate. Roll the tuna cubes in the sesame oil, followed by the sesame seeds.

Lay the nori strips out on a work surface. Roll each tuna cube in a sheet of nori, trimming off any excess so that the nori goes round the tuna once with only a little overlap. Moisten the top edge of the nori with a little water to seal the end.

Heat the vegetable oil in a large frying pan over a high heat and add the tuna cubes, standing them up on one nori-free end. Cook for 2 minutes, then turn over to cook the other nori-free end. The sesame seeds should be a dark brown, but not burnt, and the tuna should have cooked most of the way through, leaving a rare patch in the centre. If you prefer your tuna completely cooked, cook each end for a little longer. Serve hot or warm.

makes 24 | *prep* 20 minutes | *cook* 8 minutes

SEVEN-SPICED SALMON ROLLS

1 salmon fillet, about 150 g/5½ oz
sichimi togarashi (seven-spice
  powder)
dried chilli flakes, for sprinkling
1 tbsp vegetable oil
1 quantity freshly cooked Sushi Rice
6 small sheets toasted nori
2 tbsp Japanese mayonnaise

TO SERVE
shoyu (Japanese soy sauce)
wasabi paste
pickled ginger

Remove and discard the skin and bones from the salmon fillet. Dust the surface heavily with sichimi togarashi and sprinkle over a few chilli flakes. Heat the oil in a frying pan over a medium heat, add the salmon and cook on both sides for 8 minutes, or until cooked through. Leave to cool, then flake into large pieces.

Divide the rice into 6 equal portions. Lay a sheet of nori out shiny-side down on a rolling mat with the longest end towards you and, using wet hands, spread 1 portion of the rice in an even layer on the nori, leaving 2 cm/¾ inch of nori visible at the end farthest away from you. Don't squash the rice or make the layer too thick – you should be able to see the nori through the rice.

Spread the mayonnaise onto the rice at the end nearest to you. Lay one-sixth of the salmon on top of the mayonnaise.

To roll the sushi, fold the mat over, starting at the end where the ingredients are and tucking in the end of the nori to start the roll. Keep rolling, lifting up the mat as you go and keeping the pressure even but gentle until you have finished the roll. Moisten the top edge of the nori with a little water to seal the end.

Remove the roll from the mat and cut it into 4 even-sized pieces with a very sharp, wet knife. Turn the pieces on end and arrange them on a plate. Repeat with the remaining ingredients. Serve with shoyu, wasabi and pickled ginger.

makes 8–10 | *prep* 15 minutes, plus 15 minutes' chilling | *cook* no cooking required

PRESSED SUSHI BARS WITH SMOKED SALMON & CUCUMBER

vegetable oil, for oiling
1/2 quantity freshly cooked Sushi Rice
2 tbsp Japanese mayonnaise
200 g/7 oz smoked salmon
1/2 cucumber, peeled and cut into very
   thin slices

TO GARNISH
lemon wedges
handful of fresh mint sprigs

Oil an *oshi waku* or terrine tin (preferably with drop-down sides) and line it with a piece of clingfilm so that the clingfilm hangs over the edges. This is to help you lift the sushi out later. Pack the tin 3 cm/1 1/4 inches full with the rice. Spread a layer of mayonnaise on top of the rice. Arrange the smoked salmon and cucumber in diagonal strips on top of the rice, doubling up the smoked salmon layers if you have enough so that the topping is quite thick. Cover the top of the rice with a strip of clingfilm, put another terrine tin on top and weight down with a couple of food cans.

Chill the sushi in the refrigerator for 15 minutes. Remove the cans and the top tin, then lift out the sushi. Cut the sushi into 8–10 pieces with a very sharp, wet knife. Garnish with lemon wedges and mint sprigs before serving.

serves 4 | prep 10 minutes | cook 1 minute

SCATTERED SUSHI
WITH SMOKED MACKEREL

8 mangetout
5-cm/2-inch piece mooli
1 quantity freshly cooked Sushi Rice
juice and finely grated rind of 1 lemon
2 spring onions, finely chopped
2 smoked mackerel fillets, skinned,
  cut into diagonal strips
1/2 cucumber, peeled and cut
  into slices

TO GARNISH
pickled ginger
strips of toasted nori
wasabi paste

Bring a saucepan of lightly salted water to the boil, add the mangetout and blanch for 1 minute. Drain and set aside to cool. Shred the mooli using the finest setting on a mandolin or a very sharp knife. If you are using a knife, cut the mooli into long, thin slices and cut each slice along its length as finely as you can.

Mix the rice with the lemon juice and rind.

Divide the rice between 4 wooden or ceramic bowls – they should be about 2 cm/3/4 inch full. Scatter the spring onions over the top. Arrange the mackerel, cucumber, mangetout and mooli on top of the rice. Garnish with pickled ginger, nori strips and a small mound of wasabi.

serves 4 | *prep* 15 minutes | *cook* 15–30 minutes

SEAFOOD TEMPURA

8 large raw prawns, peeled and
  deveined
8 squid rings
150 g/5½ oz packet tempura mix
4 live scallops, shucked and cleaned
200 g/7 oz firm white fish fillets, cut
  into strips
vegetable oil, for deep-frying
few drops sesame oil
shoyu (Japanese soy sauce), to serve

Make little cuts on the underside of the prawns to keep them straight while they cook. Remove and discard any membranes from the squid rings.

Combine the tempura mix with the amount of water specified on the packet instructions in a large bowl until you have a lumpy batter full of air bubbles. Do not try to make the batter smooth or it will be heavy, and use it straight away or it will settle.

Drop all the seafood into the batter.

Heat the vegetable oil in a deep-fat fryer, large, heavy-based saucepan or wok to 180–190°C/350–375°F, or until a cube of bread browns in 30 seconds. Add the sesame oil.

Fry 2–3 tempura pieces at a time for 2–3 minutes until a very light golden colour (if you fry too many pieces at one time, the oil temperature will drop and the batter will be soggy). Remove with a slotted spoon and drain off as much oil as possible, then drain on kitchen paper for 30 seconds.

Serve this dish very hot with shoyu as a dipping sauce.

serves 4 | *prep* 15 minutes | *cook* 20–25 minutes

FISH FRITTERS

115 g/4 oz plain flour, plus extra
  for dusting
pinch of salt
1 egg, beaten
1 tbsp olive oil
150 ml/5 fl oz warm water
675 g/1 lb 8 oz white fish fillets, such
  as well-soaked salt cod, monkfish
  or cod
sunflower oil, for deep-frying
lemon wedges, to garnish

TO SERVE
aïoli
radishes

To make the batter, put the flour and salt in a large bowl. Make a well in the centre and pour in the egg and olive oil. Gradually add the water, beating constantly and drawing the flour from the side into the liquid, to form a smooth batter.

Remove and discard any skin and bones from the fish fillets and cut the flesh into 5-cm/ 2-inch chunks. Lightly dust with flour.

Heat the sunflower oil in a deep-fat fryer, large, heavy-based saucepan or wok to 180–190°C/350–375°F, or until a cube of bread browns in 30 seconds. Dip each fish piece into the batter to coat and fry in small batches for 5 minutes, or until crisp and golden (if you fry too many pieces at one time, the oil temperature will drop and the batter will be soggy). Remove with a slotted spoon and drain on kitchen paper.

Serve the fish fritters hot, garnished with lemon wedges and accompanied by aïoli and a bowl of radishes.

serves 4 | *prep* 10 minutes | *cook* 20 minutes

BAGNA CAUDA

6 tbsp olive oil
6 tbsp butter
4 garlic cloves, chopped
100 g/3½ oz canned anchovy fillets
  in oil, drained and chopped
6 tbsp single cream

TO SERVE
blanched asparagus spears
blanched broccoli florets
strips of red pepper
strips of pitta bread

Heat the oil in a fondue pot over a low heat, add the butter and stir until melted. Add the garlic and cook, stirring constantly, for 4 minutes.

Add the anchovies and cook, stirring frequently, for 12–15 minutes, then stir in the cream. Keep the dip warm in the fondue pot over a very low heat while you pass round a selection of asparagus, broccoli, red pepper and pitta bread strips for dipping.

makes 32 | *prep* 15 minutes | *cook* 10–15 minutes

DEVILS & ANGELS ON HORSEBACK

DEVILS
8 rindless lean bacon rashers
8 canned anchovy fillets in oil, drained
16 whole blanched almonds
16 ready-to-eat prunes

ANGELS
8 rindless lean bacon rashers
16 smoked oysters, drained if canned

Preheat the oven to 200°C/400°F/Gas Mark 6. For the devils, cut each bacon rasher lengthways in half and gently stretch with the back of a knife. Cut each anchovy fillet lengthways in half. Wrap an anchovy half around each almond and press them into the cavity where the stones have been removed from the prunes. Wrap a strip of bacon around each prune and secure with a cocktail stick.

For the angels, cut each bacon rasher lengthways in half and gently stretch with the back of a knife. Wrap a bacon strip around each oyster and secure with a cocktail stick.

Put the devils and angels onto a baking sheet and cook in the preheated oven for 10–15 minutes until sizzling hot and the bacon is cooked. Serve hot.

makes 16 | *prep* 20 minutes | *cook* 10 minutes

PRAWNS WRAPPED IN HAM

16 thin slices serrano or Parma ham
16 raw tiger prawns, peeled and
   deveined but tails left intact
extra virgin olive oil, for rubbing

TOMATO-CAPER DRESSING
2 tomatoes, peeled and deseeded
1 small red onion, very finely chopped
4 tbsp very finely chopped fresh
   parsley
1 tbsp capers, rinsed
finely grated rind of 1 large lemon
4 tbsp extra virgin olive oil
1 tbsp sherry vinegar

Preheat the oven to 160°C/325°F/
Gas Mark 3. Meanwhile, make the
dressing. Finely chop the tomato flesh and
put in a bowl. Add the onion, parsley,
capers and lemon rind and gently toss
together. Combine the oil and vinegar,
then add to the other dressing ingredients.
Mix together, cover and set aside.

Wrap a slice of ham around each prawn
and rub with a little oil. Put the prawns in a
heatproof dish large enough to hold them
in a single layer. Bake in the preheated
oven for 10 minutes.

Transfer the prawns to a serving platter
and spoon over the dressing. Serve
immediately, or leave to cool to room
temperature before serving.

serves 8 | prep 10 minutes | cook 3–4 minutes

SIZZLING CHILLI PRAWNS

500 g/1 lb 2 oz raw tiger prawns,
  in their shells
1 small fresh red chilli
6 tbsp Spanish olive oil
2 garlic cloves, finely chopped
pinch of paprika
pinch of salt
crusty bread, to serve

To prepare the prawns, pull off their heads, then peel off their shells, leaving the tails intact. Using a sharp knife, make a shallow slit along the underside of each prawn, then pull out the dark vein and discard. Rinse the prawns under cold running water and dry well on kitchen paper.

Cut the chilli in half lengthways, remove and discard the seeds and finely chop the flesh. Wear gloves while you do this or wash your hands very thoroughly afterwards, as chilli juice can cause irritation to sensitive skin, especially around the eyes, nose or mouth. Whatever you do, don't rub your eyes after touching the cut flesh of a chilli.

Heat the oil in a large, heavy-based frying pan or flameproof casserole over a medium heat, add the garlic and cook for 30 seconds, stirring. Add the prawns, chilli, paprika and salt and cook for 2–3 minutes, stirring constantly, until the prawns turn pink and begin to curl.

Serve the prawns in the cooking dish, still sizzling. Accompany with cocktail sticks, to spear the prawns, and chunks or slices of crusty bread to mop up the aromatic cooking oil.

serves 4 | *prep* 10 minutes | *cook* 4–6 minutes

SESAME PRAWN TOASTS

Put the prawns and lard on a chopping board and chop them together until they form a paste. Scrape into a bowl and stir in the egg white, spring onions, ginger and rice wine. Mix the cornflour and water together in a small bowl until a smooth paste forms, then stir into the prawn mixture and season to taste with salt and pepper.

Spread the prawn paste evenly over one side of each slice of bread. Spread out the sesame seeds on a large, flat plate or tray and gently press the spread side of each slice of bread into the seeds to coat.

Heat the oil in a preheated wok or large, heavy-based frying pan. Add half the slices of bread, spread-side down, and cook for 2–3 minutes until golden brown. Remove with a slotted spoon and drain on kitchen paper. Cook the remaining slices in the same way. Cut each slice into fingers and serve immediately.

225 g/8 oz raw prawns, peeled and
   deveined
25 g/1 oz lard
1 egg white, lightly beaten
1 tsp chopped spring onions
1/2 tsp finely chopped fresh root
   ginger
1 tbsp Chinese rice wine or dry sherry
1 tsp cornflour
2 tsp water
6 slices white bread, crusts removed
140 g/5 oz sesame seeds
groundnut oil, for deep-frying
salt and pepper

makes 25 | *prep* 15 minutes | *cook* 10–15 minutes

DEEP-FRIED PRAWN BALLS

280 g/10 oz raw prawns, peeled and
   deveined
2.5-cm/1-inch piece fresh root ginger,
   roughly chopped
225 g/8 oz beansprouts, roughly
   chopped
1 bunch of spring onions, roughly
   chopped
115 g/4 oz plain flour
1 tsp baking powder
1 egg, lightly beaten
1/2 tsp sambal oelek
pinch of salt
1–2 tbsp lukewarm water, if needed
groundnut or sunflower oil, for
   deep-frying
dip of your choice, to serve (optional)

Put the prawns, ginger, beansprouts and spring onions in a food processor and process until finely chopped, scraping down the sides of the mixing bowl once or twice. Scrape the mixture into a bowl and add the flour, baking powder, egg, sambal oelek and salt. Mix thoroughly with your hands until a firm mixture forms, adding a little of the water if necessary.

Heat the oil in a deep-fat fryer, large, heavy-based saucepan or wok to 180–190°C/350–375°F, or until a cube of bread browns in 30 seconds.

Meanwhile, shape spoonfuls of the prawn mixture into walnut-sized balls with your hands. Fry the prawn balls in small batches for 2–3 minutes until golden brown (if you fry too many balls at one time, the oil temperature will drop and they will be soggy). Remove with a slotted spoon and drain on kitchen paper. If serving hot, serve immediately, or leave to cool to room temperature. Serve with a dip, if desired.

makes 16 | *prep* 15 minutes | *cook* 5–10 minutes

TIGER PRAWNS
WITH SWEET & SOUR SAUCE

DIP
1 small red bird's-eye chilli, deseeded
1 tsp runny honey
4 tbsp soy sauce

ROLLS
2 tbsp fresh coriander leaves
1 garlic clove
1½ tsp Thai Red Curry Paste
16 wonton wrappers
1 egg white, lightly beaten
16 raw tiger prawns, peeled and
    deveined but with tails left intact
sunflower oil, for deep-frying

To make the dip, finely chop the chilli, then mix with the honey and soy in a small serving bowl and stir well. Cover and set aside.

To make the prawn rolls, finely chop the coriander and garlic, then mix with the curry paste in a bowl.

Spread the wonton wrappers out on a work surface. Brush each wonton wrapper with egg white and put a small dab of the coriander mixture in the centre. Put a prawn on top.

Fold the wonton wrapper over, enclosing the prawn and leaving the tail exposed. Repeat with the other prawns.

Heat the oil in a deep-fat fryer, large, heavy-based saucepan or wok to 180–190°C/350–375°F, or until a cube of bread browns in 30 seconds. Fry the prawns in small batches for 1–2 minutes until golden brown and crisp (if you fry too many prawns at one time, the oil temperature will drop and they will be soggy). Drain on kitchen paper and serve with the dip.

serves 8 | *prep* 30 minutes | *cook* 15 minutes

MUSSELS WITH HERB & GARLIC BUTTER

800 g/1 lb 12 oz live mussels
splash of dry white wine
1 bay leaf
85 g/3 oz butter
35 g/1¼ oz fresh white or brown
  breadcrumbs
4 tbsp chopped fresh flat-leaf parsley,
  plus extra sprigs to garnish
2 tbsp snipped fresh chives
2 garlic cloves, finely chopped
salt and pepper
lemon wedges, to serve

Preheat the oven to 230°C/450°F/Gas Mark 8. Clean the mussels by scrubbing or scraping the shells and pulling out any beards that are attached to them. Discard any with broken shells and any that refuse to close when tapped. Put the mussels in a colander and rinse well under cold running water.

Put the mussels in a large saucepan and add the wine and bay leaf. Cook, covered, over a high heat, shaking the saucepan occasionally, for 3–4 minutes, or until the mussels have opened. Discard any mussels that remain closed. Sieve the mussels.

Shell the mussels, reserving one half of each shell. Arrange the mussels, in their half shells, in a large, shallow, ovenproof serving dish.

Melt the butter in a small saucepan and pour into a small bowl. Add the breadcrumbs, parsley, chives, garlic and salt and pepper to taste and mix together well. Leave until the butter has set slightly. Using your fingers or 2 teaspoons, take a large pinch of the butter mixture and use to fill each mussel shell, pressing it down well.

Bake the mussels in the preheated oven for 10 minutes, or until hot. Serve immediately, garnished with parsley sprigs and accompanied by lemon wedges for squeezing over.

makes 16 | *prep* 20 minutes | *cook* 25–35 minutes

CARIBBEAN CRAB CAKES

1 potato, peeled and cut into chunks
pinch of salt
4 spring onions, chopped
1 garlic clove, chopped
1 tbsp chopped fresh thyme
1 tbsp chopped fresh basil
1 tbsp chopped fresh coriander
225 g/8 oz white crabmeat, drained if
   canned and thawed if frozen
1/2 tsp Dijon mustard
1/2 fresh green chilli, deseeded and
   finely chopped
1 egg, lightly beaten
plain flour, for dusting
sunflower oil, for shallow-frying
pepper
lime wedges, to garnish
dip or salsa of your choice, to serve

Put the potato in a small saucepan and add water to cover and the salt. Bring to the boil, then reduce the heat, cover and simmer for 10–15 minutes until softened. Drain well, turn into a large bowl and mash with a potato masher or fork until smooth.

Meanwhile, put the spring onions, garlic, thyme, basil and coriander in a mortar and pound with a pestle until smooth. Add the herb paste to the mashed potato with the crabmeat, mustard, chilli, egg and pepper to taste. Mix well, cover with clingfilm and chill in the refrigerator for 30 minutes.

Sprinkle flour onto a large, flat plate. Shape spoonfuls of the crabmeat mixture into small balls with your hands, then flatten slightly and dust with flour, shaking off any excess. Heat the oil in a frying pan over a high heat, add the crab cakes and cook in batches for 2–3 minutes on each side until golden. Remove with a slotted spoon and drain on kitchen paper. Set aside to cool to room temperature.

Arrange the crab cakes on a serving dish and garnish with lime wedges. Serve with a bowl of dip or salsa.

makes 24 | *prep* 20 minutes | *cook* 15 minutes

SEAFOOD FILO PARCELS

100 g/3½ oz canned red salmon,
   drained
100 g/3½ oz canned crabmeat,
   drained
2 tbsp chopped fresh parsley
8 spring onions, finely chopped
8 sheets filo pastry (about 20 x 30 cm/
   8 x 12 inches), thawed if frozen
melted butter, for brushing
sunflower oil, for oiling

Preheat the oven to 200°C/400°F/Gas Mark 6.
Remove and discard the skin and bones from
the salmon, put in a bowl and gently flake
with a fork. Remove and discard any cartilage
from the crabmeat, put in a separate bowl
and gently flake with a fork. Divide the parsley
and spring onions between the bowls and mix
well together.

Lay a sheet of filo pastry out on a work
surface, brush with melted butter, then
place a second sheet on top, keeping the
remaining sheets covered with a damp tea
towel. Cut into 10-cm/4-inch squares. Place
a teaspoonful of the salmon mixture on each
square. Brush the edges of the pastry with
melted butter, then draw together to make
little pouches. Pinch together to seal. Repeat
with 2 more sheets of filo and the salmon
mixture, then repeat with the remaining
sheets of filo and the crabmeat mixture.

Lightly oil a baking tray and put the parcels
on it. Bake in the preheated oven for
15 minutes until golden. Serve warm.

CRISPY CRAB WONTONS

To make the filling, mix the crabmeat, water chestnuts, chilli, spring onion, cornflour, sherry, soy sauce and lime juice together in a bowl.

Spread the wonton wrappers out on a work surface and spoon an equal portion of the filling into the centre of each wonton wrapper.

Dampen the edges of the wonton wrappers with a little water and fold them in half to form triangles. Fold the 2 pointed ends in towards the centre, moisten with a little water to secure, then pinch together to seal.

Heat the oil in a deep-fat fryer, large, heavy-based saucepan or wok to 180–190°C/ 350–375°F, or until a cube of bread browns in 30 seconds. Fry the wontons in batches for 2–3 minutes until golden brown and crisp (if you fry too many wontons at one time, the oil temperature will drop and they will be soggy). Remove with a slotted spoon and drain on kitchen paper.

Serve the wontons hot, garnished with lime slices.

175 g/6 oz white crabmeat, drained if canned and thawed if frozen, flaked
50 g/1³/₄ oz canned water chestnuts, drained, rinsed and chopped
1 small fresh red chilli, chopped
1 spring onion, chopped
1 tbsp cornflour
1 tsp dry sherry
1 tsp light soy sauce
¹/₂ tsp lime juice
24 wonton wrappers
vegetable oil, for deep-frying
lime slices, to garnish

3

Looking for something light and elegant to serve as a first course? Fish is the perfect solution, full of fresh, natural flavour, as well as subtle, inviting colour – especially when teamed with bright green herbs and vibrant lemon or lime wedges. And it's a winner whether the dish is simplicity itself or a little more elaborate.

FISH FIRST

Nothing could be simpler to prepare than Gravadlax – it only needs time to develop its delicious flavour. Ceviche is another refrigerator classic, which really packs a punch. But those bistro favourites Moules Marinière, Calamares and Thai Fish Cakes are hard to beat. However, if you are out to impress, Salmon Tartare is seriously sophisticated, Noodle-wrapped Teriyaki Fish stylish and Chèvre & Oyster Tartlets outrageously upmarket.

serves 8 | *prep* 10 minutes | *cook* 15 minutes

SMOKED FISH PATE

900 g/2 lb undyed kipper fillets
2 garlic cloves, finely chopped
175 ml/6 fl oz olive oil
6 tbsp single cream
salt and pepper
lemon slices, to garnish
oatcakes, to serve

Put the kippers in a large frying pan or fish kettle and add cold water to just cover. Bring to the boil, then immediately reduce the heat and poach gently for 10 minutes until tender. If using a frying pan, you may need to do this in batches.

Transfer the fish to a chopping board using a fish slice. Remove and discard the skin. Roughly flake the flesh with a fork and remove and discard any remaining tiny bones. Transfer the fish to a saucepan over a low heat, add the garlic and break up the fish with a wooden spoon.

Gradually add the oil, beating well after each addition. Add the cream and beat until smooth, but do not allow the mixture to boil.

Remove the saucepan from the heat and season to taste with salt, if necessary, and pepper. Spoon the pâté into a serving dish, cover and set aside to cool completely. Chill in the refrigerator until required, for up to 3 days.

Garnish with lemon slices and serve with oatcakes.

makes 4 | *prep* 10 minutes | *cook* 20–25 minutes

TUNA STUFFED TOMATOES

4 plum tomatoes
2 tbsp sun-dried tomato paste
115 g/4 oz canned tuna, drained
2 tbsp capers, rinsed
salt and pepper

MAYONNAISE
2 egg yolks
2 tsp lemon juice
finely grated rind of 1 lemon
4 tbsp olive oil

TO GARNISH
2 sun-dried tomatoes, cut into strips
fresh basil leaves

Preheat the oven to 200°C/400°F/Gas Mark 6. Halve the fresh tomatoes, scoop out the seeds and discard. Divide the sun-dried tomato paste between the tomato halves and spread around the inside of the tomato shells.

Put on a baking tray and roast in the preheated oven for 12–15 minutes. Leave to cool slightly.

Meanwhile, make the mayonnaise. Put the egg yolks and lemon juice and rind in a blender or food processor and process until smooth. With the motor running, very slowly add the oil through the feed tube. Stop the machine as soon as the mayonnaise has thickened. Alternatively, use a hand whisk, beating the mixture constantly until it thickens.

Flake the tuna with a fork, then stir into the mayonnaise with the capers and salt and pepper to taste.

Spoon the tuna mayonnaise mixture into the tomato shells and garnish with sun-dried tomato strips and basil leaves. Return to the oven for a few minutes to heat through before serving or serve chilled.

serves 8–12 | *prep* 10 minutes, plus 2 days' chilling | *cook* no cooking required

GRAVADLAX

Rinse the salmon fillets under cold running water and dry with kitchen paper. Put 1 fillet, skin-side down, in a non-metallic dish.

Mix the dill, sea salt, sugar and peppercorns together in a small bowl. Spread this mixture over the fillet in the dish and put the second fillet, skin-side up, on top. Put a plate, the same size as the fish, on top and weight down with 3–4 food cans.

Chill in the refrigerator for 2 days, turning the fish about every 12 hours and basting with any juices that come out of the fish.

Remove the salmon from the brine and thinly slice, without slicing the skin, as you would smoked salmon. Cut the buttered bread into triangles and serve with the salmon. Garnish with lemon wedges and dill sprigs.

2 salmon fillets, with skin on, about
   450 g/1 lb each
6 tbsp roughly chopped fresh dill
115 g/4 oz sea salt
50 g/1¾ oz sugar
1 tbsp white peppercorns, roughly
   crushed
12 slices brown bread, buttered,
   to serve

TO GARNISH
lemon slices
fresh dill sprigs

serves 4 | prep 15 minutes, plus 30 minutes' chilling | cook 20 minutes

THAI FISH CAKES

500 g/1 lb 2 oz skinless, boneless
    cod fillet, cut into chunks
1 tbsp Thai Red Curry Paste
1 egg, beaten
1 tsp light muscovado sugar
1 tsp salt
1 tbsp cornflour
75 g/2¾ oz French beans,
    finely chopped
1 tbsp chopped fresh coriander
4 tbsp vegetable oil
lime wedges, to garnish

TO SERVE
salad
stir-fried green vegetables,
    such as French beans, broccoli
    and mangetout

Put the cod in a food processor and process until roughly chopped. Add the curry paste, egg, sugar, salt and cornflour and process until well blended.

Stir in the beans and coriander.

Transfer to a bowl, cover with clingfilm and chill in the refrigerator for 30 minutes.

Remove from the refrigerator, shape the fish mixture into 12 balls with your hands, then flatten each ball into a 5-cm/2-inch cake.

Heat the oil in a frying pan over a medium heat, add the fish cakes and cook in batches for 3 minutes on each side, or until golden brown and cooked through. Keep warm in a low oven while cooking the remainder.

Garnish with lime wedges and serve with salad or stir-fried green vegetables such as French beans, mangetout or broccoli.

serves 4 | *prep* 15 minutes, plus 20 minutes' chilling | *cook* 20 minutes

NOODLE-WRAPPED TERIYAKI FISH

2 boneless salmon steaks, about
   175 g/6 oz each and about 2 cm/
   ³/₄ inch thick, skinned
bottled or home-made teriyaki sauce
12 large spinach leaves, rinsed
   and dried with any tough stems
   removed, or about 36 young
   spinach leaves
48 long, fresh medium Chinese
   egg noodles

Using a sharp knife, cut the salmon steaks into 2.5-cm/1-inch pieces.

Brush the top of each fish piece with teriyaki sauce. Working with 1 spinach leaf at a time, lay it out on a work surface, bottom-side up, with the stem end facing you. Place a piece of fish, sauce-side down, in the centre of the leaf. Fold the sides inwards to overlap, then roll up from the bottom so that the fish is enclosed. Continue wrapping the remaining fish pieces. Wrap each spinach parcel with 2 noodles, from side to side, then repeat with 2 more noodles, wrapped at right angles. Have all the dangling loose noodle ends on the bottom, then cut off the excess and press the ends together. Cover and chill in the refrigerator for at least 20 minutes or up to 8 hours.

To cook, place a bamboo steamer over a saucepan of boiling water. Put as many fish parcels as will fit in a single layer in the steamer, cover and steam for 10 minutes. Serve immediately, while you steam any remaining parcels.

serves 4 | prep 20 minutes, plus 48 hours' marinating | cook no cooking required

SALMON TARTARE

Put the salmon in a shallow non-metallic dish. Combine the sea salt, sugar and chopped dill in a small bowl, then rub the mixture into the fish until well coated. Season to taste with pepper. Cover with clingfilm and chill in the refrigerator for at least 48 hours, turning the salmon once.

Put the tarragon in a bowl with the mustard, lemon juice and salt and pepper to taste. Remove the salmon from the refrigerator, chop into small pieces and add to the bowl. Stir until the salmon is well coated.

To make the topping, put all the topping ingredients in a separate bowl and mix well together. Put a 10-cm/4-inch steel cooking ring or round biscuit cutter on each of 4 small serving plates. Divide the salmon between the 4 steel rings so that each ring is half full. Level the surface of each one, then top with the cream cheese mixture. Smooth the surfaces, then carefully remove the steel rings. Garnish with dill sprigs and serve.

500 g/1 lb 2 oz salmon fillet, skinned
2 tbsp sea salt
1 tbsp caster sugar
2 tbsp chopped fresh dill, plus extra
    sprigs to garnish
1 tbsp chopped fresh tarragon
1 tsp Dijon mustard
juice of 1 lemon
salt and pepper

TOPPING
400 g/14 oz cream cheese
1 tbsp snipped fresh chives
pinch of paprika

serves 4–6 | *prep* 15 minutes, plus 1–2 hours' marinating | *cook* 10 minutes

MONKFISH, ROSEMARY & BACON SKEWERS

350 g/12 oz monkfish tail or 250 g/
   9 oz monkfish fillet
12 fresh rosemary stems
3 tbsp Spanish olive oil
juice of 1/2 small lemon
1 garlic clove, crushed
6 rindless thick back bacon rashers
salt and pepper
lemon wedges, to garnish
aïoli, to serve

If using monkfish tail, cut either side of the central bone with a sharp knife and remove the flesh to form 2 fillets. Slice the fillets in half lengthways, then cut each fillet into 12 bite-sized chunks to give a total of 24 pieces. Put the monkfish pieces in a large bowl.

To prepare the rosemary skewers, strip the leaves off the stems and reserve them, leaving a few leaves at one end.

For the marinade, finely chop the reserved leaves and whisk with the oil, lemon juice, garlic and salt and pepper to taste in a non-metallic bowl. Add the monkfish pieces and toss until coated in the marinade. Cover and leave to marinate in the refrigerator for 1–2 hours.

Cut each bacon rasher in half lengthways, then in half widthways, and roll up each piece. Thread 2 monkfish pieces alternately with 2 bacon rolls onto the prepared rosemary skewers.

Preheat the grill, griddle or barbecue. If you are cooking the skewers under an overhead grill, arrange them on the grill rack so that the leaves of the rosemary skewers protrude from the grill and therefore do not catch fire during cooking. Cook the monkfish and bacon skewers, turning frequently and basting with any remaining marinade, for 10 minutes, or until cooked. Serve hot, garnished with lemon wedges for squeezing over and accompanied by a bowl of aïoli for dipping.

serves 4 | *prep* 10 minutes, plus 30 minutes' chilling | *cook* no cooking required

PRAWN COCKTAIL

Divide the lettuce between 4 small serving dishes (traditionally, stemmed glass ones, but any small dishes will be fine).

Mix the mayonnaise, cream and tomato ketchup together in a bowl. Add the Tabasco sauce and lemon juice and season well with salt and pepper.

Divide the peeled prawns equally between the dishes and pour over the dressing. Cover and chill in the refrigerator for 30 minutes.

Sprinkle a little paprika over the cocktails and garnish each dish with a prawn and a lemon slice. Serve the cocktails with slices of brown bread and butter.

½ iceberg lettuce, finely shredded
150 ml/5 fl oz mayonnaise
2 tbsp single cream
2 tbsp tomato ketchup
few drops of Tabasco sauce,
  or to taste
juice of ½ lemon, or to taste
175 g/6 oz cooked peeled prawns
salt and pepper
thin buttered brown bread slices,
  to serve

TO GARNISH
paprika, for sprinkling
4 cooked prawns, in their shells
4 lemon slices

serves 4 | *prep* 15 minutes, plus 8 hours' marinating | *cook* 8–12 minutes

PRAWN SATAY

12 raw king prawns, peeled but with
   tails left intact

MARINADE
1 tsp ground coriander
1 tsp ground cumin
2 tbsp light soy sauce
4 tbsp vegetable oil
1 tbsp curry powder
1 tbsp ground turmeric
125 ml/4 fl oz canned coconut milk
3 tbsp sugar

PEANUT SAUCE
2 tbsp vegetable oil
3 garlic cloves, crushed
1 tbsp Thai Red Curry Paste
125 ml/4 fl oz canned coconut milk
225 ml/8 fl oz fish or chicken stock
1 tbsp sugar
1 tsp salt
1 tbsp lemon juice
4 tbsp unsalted roasted peanuts,
   finely chopped
4 tbsp dried white breadcrumbs

Using a sharp knife, make a shallow slit along the underside of each prawn, then pull out the dark vein and discard. Set aside. Mix the marinade ingredients together in a bowl and add the prawns. Mix well together, cover and leave to marinate in the refrigerator for at least 8 hours or overnight.

To make the sauce, heat the oil in a large frying pan over a high heat. Add the garlic and cook, stirring, until just starting to colour. Add the curry paste and cook, stirring, for a further 30 seconds. Add the coconut milk, stock, sugar, salt and lemon juice and stir well. Boil for 1–2 minutes, stirring constantly. Add the peanuts and breadcrumbs and mix well together. Pour into a bowl, cover and set aside.

Preheat the grill or barbecue. Thread 3 prawns onto each of 4 skewers. Cook under or over a high heat for 3–4 minutes on each side until just cooked through. Serve immediately with the peanut sauce.

serves 4 | *prep* 25 minutes | *cook* 5 minutes

MOULES MARINIERE

2 kg/4 lb 8 oz live mussels
300 ml/10 fl oz dry white wine
6 shallots, finely chopped
1 bouquet garni
pepper
crusty bread, to serve

Clean the mussels by scrubbing or scraping the shells and pulling out any beards that are attached to them. Discard any with broken shells or any that refuse to close when tapped. Put the mussels in a colander and rinse well under cold running water.

Pour the wine into a large, heavy-based saucepan, add the shallots and bouquet garni and season to taste with pepper. Bring to the boil over a medium heat. Add the mussels, cover tightly and cook, shaking the saucepan occasionally, for 3–4 minutes, or until the mussels have opened. Remove and discard the bouquet garni and any mussels that remain closed.

Divide the mussels between 4 soup plates with a slotted spoon. Tilt the saucepan to let any sand settle, then spoon the cooking liquid over the mussels. Serve immediately with bread.

serves 4 | *prep* 25 minutes, plus 2 hours' chilling | *cook* no cooking required

CEVICHE

8 live scallops, shucked
16 large raw prawns, in shells
2 sea bass fillets, about 150 g/5½ oz
    each, skinned
1 large lemon
1 lime
1 red onion, thinly sliced
½ fresh red chilli, deseeded and finely
    chopped
2–4 tbsp extra virgin olive oil

TO SERVE
salad leaves
lime or lemon wedges
pepper

Scrub the scallops under cold running water. Using a strong knife, prise the shells open. Remove and discard the grey beard that surrounds each scallop and the black thread and stomach bag. Detach the scallop and coral from each shell with a spoon and separate the coral from the scallop. Rinse under cold running water and dry with kitchen paper. Slice the scallops into 2–3 horizontal slices each, depending on the size. Put in a non-metallic bowl with the corals.

Pull off the heads of the prawns, then peel off their shells. Using a sharp knife, make a shallow slit in the underside of each prawn, then pull out the dark vein and discard. Rinse the prawns under cold running water and dry well on kitchen paper. Add to the scallops.

Cut the sea bass into thin slices across the grain and add to the shellfish.

Cut the lemon in half and squeeze the juice over the fish. Repeat with the lime.

Gently stir to coat the seafood well in the citrus juices, then cover and chill in the refrigerator for 2 hours, or until the seafood becomes opaque, but do not leave for longer or the seafood will be too soft.

Using a slotted spoon, transfer the seafood to a separate bowl. Add the onion, chilli and oil and gently stir together. Leave to stand for 5 minutes.

Spoon onto individual plates and serve with salad leaves, lemon or lime wedges and pepper.

makes 12 | *prep* 20 minutes, plus 45 minutes' chilling | *cook* 20 minutes

CHEVRE & OYSTER TARTLETS

125 g/4½ oz plain flour, plus extra
  for dusting
pinch of salt
100 g/3½ oz butter, diced, plus extra
  for greasing
1 egg yolk
1 onion, chopped
12 live oysters, shucked
2 tbsp chopped fresh flat-leaf parsley,
  plus extra sprigs to garnish
salt and pepper
200 g/7 oz goat's cheese, crumbled

Grease 12 x 7-cm/2¾-inch tartlet tins. Sift the flour and salt together into a bowl. Rub 90 g/3¼ oz of the butter into the flour until fine crumbs form. Mix in the egg yolk to make a dough. Add a little cold water if needed. Shape into a ball and turn out onto a lightly floured work surface. Roll out to a thickness of 5 mm/¼ inch. Line the prepared tins with the pastry and trim the edges. Cover and chill in the refrigerator for 45 minutes.

Preheat the oven to 200°C/400°F/Gas Mark 6. Remove the tartlet cases from the refrigerator and bake in the preheated oven for 10 minutes until golden.

Meanwhile, heat the remaining butter in a saucepan over a medium heat, add the onion and cook, stirring frequently for 4 minutes. Add the oysters, parsley and salt and pepper to taste and cook, stirring, for 1 minute.

Remove the tartlet cases from the oven. Divide half of the goat's cheese between them. Top with the oyster mixture, crumble over the remaining cheese, then bake for a further 10 minutes. Garnish with parsley sprigs and serve hot.

serves 8 | *prep* 25 minutes | *cook* 35 minutes

SCALLOPS IN SAFFRON SAUCE

150 ml/5 fl oz dry white wine
150 ml/5 fl oz fish stock
large pinch of saffron threads
900 g/2 lb shucked live scallops,
   preferably large ones
3 tbsp Spanish olive oil
1 small onion, finely chopped
2 garlic cloves, finely chopped
150 ml/5 fl oz double cream
squeeze of lemon juice
salt and pepper
chopped fresh flat-leaf parsley,
   to garnish
crusty bread, to serve

Put the wine, stock and saffron in a saucepan over a medium heat and bring to the boil. Reduce the heat, cover and simmer gently for 15 minutes.

Remove and discard the grey beard that surrounds each scallop and the black thread and stomach bag. Detach the scallop and coral from each shell with a spoon. Rinse under cold running water and dry with kitchen paper. Slice the scallops horizontally into thick slices, including the corals. Season to taste with salt and pepper.

Heat the oil in a large, heavy-based frying pan over a medium heat. Add the onion and garlic and cook, stirring frequently, for 5 minutes, or until softened and lightly browned. Add the sliced scallops and cook gently, stirring occasionally, for 5 minutes, or until they just turn opaque. Do not overcook the scallops or they will become tough and rubbery.

Using a slotted spoon, transfer the scallops to a warmed plate. Add the saffron liquid to the pan, bring to the boil and boil rapidly until reduced by about half. Reduce the heat and gradually stir in the cream, just a little at a time. Simmer gently until the sauce thickens.

Return the scallops to the pan and simmer in the sauce for 1–2 minutes just to heat them through. Add the lemon juice and season to taste with salt and pepper. Serve the scallops hot, garnished with chopped parsley and accompanied by chunks or slices of crusty bread to mop up the saffron sauce.

serves 4–6 | *prep* 10–25 minutes, plus 1–2 hours' chilling | *cook* 10 minutes

POTTED CRAB

1 large cooked crab, prepared
  if possible
whole nutmeg, for grating
2 pinches of cayenne pepper or mace
juice of 1 lemon, or to taste
225 g/8 oz lightly salted butter
salt and pepper

TO SERVE
buttered toast slices
lemon wedges

If the crab is not already prepared, pick out all the white and brown meat, taking great care to remove all the meat from the claws.

Mix the white and brown meat together in a bowl, but do not mash too smoothly. Season well with salt and pepper and add a good grating of nutmeg, the cayenne pepper and lemon juice.

Melt half the butter in a saucepan over a medium heat and carefully stir in the crabmeat. Turn the mixture out into 4–6 small soufflé dishes or ramekins.

Melt the remaining butter in a clean saucepan over a medium heat, then continue heating for a few moments until it stops bubbling. Allow the sediment to settle, then carefully pour the clarified butter over the crab mixture. Cover and chill in the refrigerator for at least an hour before serving with buttered toast and lemon wedges. The seal of clarified butter allows the potted crab to be kept for 1–2 days.

serves 6 | *prep* 10 minutes | *cook* 8–12 minutes

CALAMARES

450 g/1 lb prepared squid
plain flour, for coating
sunflower oil, for deep-frying
salt
lemon wedges, to garnish
aïoli, to serve

Slice the squid into 1-cm/$\frac{1}{2}$-inch rings and halve the tentacles if large. Rinse under cold running water and dry well with kitchen paper. Dust the squid rings with flour so that they are lightly coated.

Heat the oil in a deep-fat fryer, large, heavy-based saucepan or wok to 180–190°C/ 350–375°F, or until a cube of bread browns in 30 seconds. Fry the squid rings in small batches for 2–3 minutes, or until golden brown and crisp all over, turning several times (if you fry too many squid rings at one time, the oil temperature will drop and they will be soggy). Do not overcook as the squid will become tough and rubbery rather than moist and tender.

Remove with a slotted spoon and drain well on kitchen paper. Keep warm in a low oven while you fry the remaining squid rings.

Sprinkle the fried squid rings with salt and serve piping hot, garnished with lemon wedges for squeezing over. Accompany with a bowl of aïoli for dipping.

4

When it comes to soups and stews, fish's famed diversity and versatility really come into their own. Fish offers the whole range of eating experience, from the smooth, creamy and subtly flavoured to the hearty, chunky and spicy, with all the glorious variations in between. And all this cooked in one pot and served in one bowl!

SOUPS AND STEWS

The recipe titles in this chapter read like a Who's Who of the world's great cuisines – New England Clam Chowder, Bouillabaisse, Louisiana Gumbo, Sweetcorn & Crab Soup and Prawn Laksa. But there are other, less well-known regional delights besides – Spanish Swordfish Stew, Mexican Fish & Roasted Tomato Soup and the fragrant Breton Fish Soup with Cider & Sorrel.

serves 4 | *prep* 15 minutes, plus 30 minutes' marinating | *cook* 40 minutes

COD & SWEET POTATO SOUP

4 tbsp lemon juice
1 fresh red chilli, deseeded and
   finely sliced
pinch of nutmeg
250 g/9 oz cod fillets, skinned, rinsed
   and dried
1 tbsp vegetable oil
1 onion, chopped
4 spring onions, chopped
2 garlic cloves, chopped
450 g/1 lb sweet potatoes, diced
1 litre/1¾ pints vegetable stock
1 carrot, sliced
150 g/5½ oz white cabbage,
   shredded
2 celery sticks, sliced
salt and pepper
crusty bread, **to serve**

Put the lemon juice, chilli and nutmeg in a shallow, non-metallic dish and mix together. Cut the cod into chunks and add to the dish. Turn in the marinade until well coated. Cover with clingfilm and leave to marinate in the refrigerator for 30 minutes.

Heat the oil in a large saucepan over a medium heat. Add the onion and spring onions and cook, stirring frequently, for 4 minutes. Add the garlic and cook, stirring, for 2 minutes.

Add the sweet potatoes, stock and salt and pepper to taste. Bring to the boil, then reduce the heat, cover and simmer for 10 minutes. Add the carrot, cabbage and celery, season again and simmer for 8–10 minutes.

Leave the soup to cool slightly, then transfer to a blender or food processor and process until smooth, working in batches if necessary. Return to the saucepan. Add the fish and marinade and bring gently to the boil. Reduce the heat and simmer for 10 minutes. Ladle the soup into bowls and serve with crusty bread.

serves 4 | *prep* 15 minutes | *cook* 30–35 minutes

GARLIC FISH SOUP

2 tsp olive oil
1 large onion, chopped
1 small fennel bulb, chopped
1 leek, sliced
3–4 large garlic cloves, thinly sliced
125 ml/4 fl oz dry white wine
1.2 litres/2 pints fish stock
4 tbsp white rice
1 strip of thinly pared lemon rind
1 bay leaf
450 g/1 lb skinless white fish fillets,
    cut into 4-cm/1½-inch pieces
50 ml/2 fl oz double cream
salt and pepper
2 tbsp chopped fresh parsley, to
    garnish

Heat the oil in a large saucepan over a medium–low heat. Add the onion, fennel, leek and garlic and cook, stirring frequently, for 4–5 minutes until the onion is softened.

Add the wine and let the mixture bubble briefly. Add the stock, rice, lemon rind and bay leaf. Bring to the boil, then reduce the heat to medium–low and simmer for 20–25 minutes until the rice and vegetables are soft. Remove and discard the lemon rind and bay leaf.

Leave the soup to cool slightly, then transfer to a blender or food processor and process until smooth, working in batches if necessary. (If using a food processor, strain off the cooking liquid and reserve. Purée the solids with enough cooking liquid to moisten them, then combine with the remaining liquid.)

Return the soup to the saucepan and bring to a simmer. Add the fish to the soup, cover and let simmer gently, stirring occasionally, for a further 4–5 minutes until the fish is cooked and begins to flake.

Stir in the cream. Taste and adjust the seasoning, adding salt, if necessary, and pepper. Ladle into warmed bowls and serve sprinkled with chopped parsley.

serves 4 | *prep* 15 minutes | *cook* 35 minutes

BRETON FISH SOUP
WITH CIDER & SORREL

2 tsp butter
1 large leek, thinly sliced
2 shallots, finely chopped
125 ml/4 fl oz dry cider
300 ml/10 fl oz fish stock
250 g/9 oz potatoes, diced
1 bay leaf
4 tbsp plain flour
200 ml/7 fl oz milk
200 ml/7 fl oz double cream
55 g/2 oz sorrel leaves
350 g/12 oz skinless monkfish or cod
  fillets, cut into 2.5-cm/1-inch pieces
salt and pepper

Melt the butter in a large saucepan over a medium–low heat. Add the leek and shallots and cook, stirring frequently, for 5 minutes, or until they start to soften. Add the cider and bring to the boil.

Stir in the stock, potatoes and bay leaf with a large pinch of salt (unless the stock is salty) and return to the boil. Reduce the heat, cover and cook gently for 10 minutes.

Put the flour in a small bowl and very slowly whisk in a few tablespoons of the milk to make a thick paste. Stir in a little more milk to make a smooth liquid.

Adjust the heat so that the soup bubbles gently. Stir in the flour mixture and cook, stirring frequently, for 5 minutes. Add the remaining milk and half the cream. Cook for a further 10 minutes, or until the potatoes are tender.

Finely chop the sorrel and combine with the remaining cream. (If using a food processor, add the sorrel and chop, then add the cream and process briefly.)

Stir the sorrel cream into the soup and add the fish. Cook, stirring occasionally, for a further 3 minutes, or until the monkfish stiffens or the cod just begins to flake. Taste the soup and adjust the seasoning, if necessary. Ladle into warmed bowls and serve.

serves 4 | *prep* 15 minutes | *cook* 35 minutes

SAFFRON FISH SOUP

2 tsp butter
1 onion, finely chopped
1 leek, thinly sliced
1 carrot, thinly sliced
pinch of saffron threads
4 tbsp white rice
125 ml/4 fl oz dry white wine
1 litre/1³⁄₄ pints fish stock
125 ml/4 fl oz double cream
350 g/12 oz skinless white fish fillets,
   such as cod, haddock or monkfish,
   cut into 1-cm/¹⁄₂-inch cubes
4 tomatoes, peeled, deseeded
   and chopped
salt and pepper
3 tbsp snipped fresh chives, to garnish

Melt the butter in a saucepan over a medium heat, add the onion, leek and carrot and cook, stirring frequently, for 3–4 minutes until the onion is softened.

Add the saffron, rice, wine and stock and bring just to the boil, then reduce the heat to low. Season to taste with salt and pepper. Cover and simmer for 20 minutes, or until the rice and vegetables are tender.

Leave the soup to cool slightly, then transfer to a blender or food processor and process until smooth, working in batches if necessary. (If using a food processor, strain off the cooking liquid and reserve. Purée the solids with enough cooking liquid to moisten them, then combine with the remaining liquid.)

Return to the saucepan, stir in the cream and simmer over a low heat for a few minutes until heated through, stirring occasionally.

Season the fish to taste with salt and pepper and add to the soup with the tomatoes. Cook for 3–5 minutes until the fish is just tender.

Stir in most of the chives. Taste the soup and adjust the seasoning, if necessary. Ladle into warmed shallow bowls, sprinkle the remaining chives on top and serve.

serves 4 | *prep* 10 minutes | *cook* 25–30 minutes

MEXICAN FISH & ROASTED TOMATO SOUP

5 ripe tomatoes
5 garlic cloves, unpeeled
1 litre/1³/₄ pints fish stock
500 g/1 lb 2 oz red snapper fillets,
  skinned and cut into chunks
2–3 tbsp olive oil
1 onion, chopped
2 fresh chillies, deseeded and
  thinly sliced
lime wedges, to serve

Heat a dry, heavy-based frying pan over a high heat, add the tomatoes and garlic cloves and cook, turning frequently, for 10–15 minutes until the skins are blackened and charred and the flesh is tender, or cook under a preheated hot grill. Alternatively, put the tomatoes and garlic cloves in a roasting tin and bake in a preheated oven at 190–200°C/375–400°F/Gas Mark 5–6 for 40 minutes.

Leave the tomatoes and garlic to cool, then remove and discard the skins and roughly chop the flesh, combining it with any juices from the pan. Set aside.

Heat the stock in a saucepan over a medium heat until simmering, add the snapper and cook just until opaque and slightly firm. Remove from the heat and set aside.

Heat the oil in a separate saucepan, add the onion and cook, stirring frequently, for 5 minutes until softened. Strain in the fish cooking liquid, then add the tomatoes and garlic and stir well.

Bring to the boil, then reduce the heat and simmer for 5 minutes to combine the flavours. Add the chillies.

Divide chunks of the poached fish between 4 soup bowls, ladle over the hot soup and serve with lime wedges for squeezing over.

serves 4–6 | prep 15 minutes | cook 1 hour

TROUT & CELERIAC SOUP

700 g/1 lb 9 oz whole trout, cleaned
200 g/7 oz celeriac, peeled and diced
150 ml/5 fl oz double cream
3 tbsp cornflour, dissolved in
  3 tbsp water
chopped fresh chervil or parsley,
  to garnish

FISH STOCK BASE
1 tbsp butter
I onion, thinly sliced
I carrot, thinly sliced
I leek, thinly sliced
225 ml/8 fl oz dry white wine
1.2 litres/2 pints water
1 bay leaf

To make the fish stock base, melt the butter in a fish kettle, a large saucepan or cast-iron casserole over a medium–high heat, add the onion, carrot and leek and cook for 3 minutes, or until the onion starts to soften.

Add the wine, water and bay leaf. Bring to the boil, then reduce the heat a little, cover and boil gently for 15 minutes.

Add the fish (cut the fish into pieces to fit, if necessary). Return to the boil and skim off any foam that rises to the surface. Reduce the heat to low and simmer gently for 20 minutes.

Remove the fish with a slotted spoon and set aside. Sieve the stock through a muslin-lined sieve into a clean saucepan. Remove any fat from the stock. (There should be about 1.5 litres/2¾ pints of stock.)

Bring the stock to the boil. Add the celeriac and boil gently, uncovered, for 15–20 minutes until it is tender and the liquid has reduced by about one third.

When the fish is cool enough to handle, peel off the skin and remove the flesh from the bones. Discard the skin, bones, head and tail.

Add the cream to the soup and return to the boil. Stir in the dissolved cornflour and boil gently, stirring frequently, for 2–3 minutes until slightly thickened. Return the fish to the soup and cook for 3–4 minutes to reheat. Taste and adjust the seasoning, if necessary. Ladle into warmed bowls and garnish with chervil or parsley.

serves 4 | *prep* 20 minutes | *cook* 15 minutes

THAI PRAWN & SCALLOP SOUP

1 litre/1³/₄ pints fish stock
juice of ¹/₂ lime
2 tbsp rice wine or sherry
1 leek, sliced
2 shallots, finely chopped
1 tbsp grated fresh root ginger
1 fresh red chilli, deseeded and finely
   chopped
225 g/8 oz raw prawns, peeled and
   deveined
225 g/8 oz live scallops, shucked and
   cleaned
1¹/₂ tbsp chopped fresh flat-leaf
   parsley, plus extra to garnish
salt and pepper

Put the stock, lime juice, rice wine, leek, shallots, ginger and chilli in a large saucepan. Bring to the boil over a high heat, then reduce the heat, cover and simmer for 10 minutes.

Add the prawns, scallops and parsley, season to taste with salt and pepper and cook for 1–2 minutes.

Remove the saucepan from the heat and ladle the soup into warmed serving bowls. Garnish with chopped parsley and serve.

serves 4 | prep 15 minutes, plus 10 minutes' cooling | cook 35 minutes

PRAWN & VEGETABLE BISQUE

3 tbsp butter
1 garlic clove, chopped
1 onion, sliced
1 carrot, chopped
1 celery stick, sliced
1.2 litres/2 pints fish stock
4 tbsp red wine
1 tbsp tomato purée
1 bay leaf
600 g/1 lb 5 oz raw prawns, peeled
  and deveined
100 ml/3½ fl oz double cream, plus
  extra to garnish
salt and pepper
cooked prawns, in their shells,
  to garnish

Melt the butter in a large saucepan over a medium heat. Add the garlic and onion and cook, stirring, for 3 minutes, until slightly softened. Add the carrot and celery and cook for a further 3 minutes, stirring. Pour in the stock and wine, then add the tomato purée and bay leaf. Season to taste with salt and pepper. Bring to the boil, then reduce the heat and simmer for 20 minutes. Remove from the heat and leave to cool for 10 minutes, then remove and discard the bay leaf.

Transfer half the soup to a blender or food processor and process until smooth, working in batches if necessary. Return to the saucepan with the remaining soup. Stir in the peeled prawns and cook over a low heat for 5–6 minutes.

Stir in the cream and cook for a further 2 minutes, then remove from the heat and ladle into warmed serving bowls. Garnish with swirls of cream and prawns. Serve immediately.

serves 4 | *prep* 15 minutes | *cook* 30 minutes

MUSSEL SOUP

750 g/1 lb 10 oz live mussels,
  scrubbed and debearded
2 tbsp olive oil
100 g/3¹/₂ oz butter
55 g/2 oz rindless streaky
  bacon, chopped
1 onion, chopped
2 garlic cloves, finely chopped
55 g/2 oz plain flour
3 potatoes, thinly sliced
115 g/4 oz dried farfalle
300 ml/10 fl oz double cream or
  panna da cucina
1 tbsp lemon juice
2 egg yolks
salt and pepper
2 tbsp finely chopped fresh parsley,
  to garnish

Bring a large, heavy-based saucepan of water to the boil over a high heat. Add the mussels, oil and pepper to taste. Cover tightly and cook, shaking the saucepan occasionally, for 3–4 minutes, or until the mussels have opened. Remove the mussels with a slotted spoon, discarding any that remain closed. Sieve the cooking liquid and reserve 1.2 litres/2 pints. Remove the mussels from their shells and reserve until required.

Melt the butter in a clean saucepan over a low heat, add the bacon, onion and garlic and cook, stirring occasionally, for 5 minutes. Stir in the flour and cook, stirring constantly, for 1 minute. Gradually stir in all but 2 tablespoons of the reserved mussel cooking liquid and bring to the boil, stirring constantly. Add the potato slices and simmer for 5 minutes. Add the pasta and simmer for a further 10 minutes.

Stir in the cream and lemon juice and season to taste with salt and pepper. Add the mussels. Mix the egg yolks and the remaining mussel cooking liquid together in a jug, then stir the mixture into the soup and cook for 4 minutes, or until thickened.

Ladle the soup into warmed soup bowls, garnish with chopped parsley and serve immediately.

serves 4 | *prep* 10 minutes | *cook* 6–8 minutes

SWEETCORN & CRAB SOUP

2 tbsp vegetable or groundnut oil
4 garlic cloves, finely chopped
5 shallots, finely chopped
2 lemon grass stalks, finely chopped
2.5-cm/1-inch piece fresh root ginger,
  finely chopped
1 litre/1¾ pints chicken stock
400 g/14 oz canned coconut milk
225 g/8 oz frozen sweetcorn kernels
350 g/12 oz canned crabmeat,
  drained and flaked
2 tbsp Thai fish sauce
juice of 1 lime
1 tsp palm sugar or soft light
  brown sugar
bunch of fresh coriander, chopped,
  to garnish

Heat the oil in a large frying pan over a low heat, add the garlic, shallots, lemon grass and ginger and cook, stirring occasionally, for 2–3 minutes until softened. Add the stock and coconut milk and bring to the boil. Add the sweetcorn, reduce the heat and simmer gently for 3–4 minutes.

Add the crabmeat, fish sauce, lime juice and sugar and simmer gently for 1 minute. Ladle into warmed bowls, garnish with the chopped coriander and serve immediately.

serves 4 | *prep* 15 minutes | *cook* 40 minutes

HADDOCK & POTATO SOUP

Melt the butter in a large saucepan over a medium heat, add the onion and leek and cook, stirring frequently, for 3 minutes, or until slightly softened. Mix the flour in a bowl with enough of the milk to make a smooth paste, then stir into the saucepan. Cook, stirring constantly, for 2 minutes, then gradually stir in the remaining milk. Add the bay leaf and parsley and season to taste with salt and pepper. Bring to the boil, then reduce the heat and simmer for 15 minutes.

Rinse the haddock fillets under cold running water, drain, then cut into bite-sized chunks. Add to the soup and cook for 15 minutes, or until the fish is tender and cooked right through. Add the mashed potatoes and stir in the cream. Cook for a further 2–3 minutes, then remove from the heat and remove and discard the bay leaf.

Ladle into warmed serving bowls, garnish with chopped parsley and serve with crusty rolls and a green salad.

2 tbsp butter
1 onion, chopped
1 leek, chopped
2 tbsp plain flour
850 ml/1½ pints milk
1 bay leaf
2 tbsp chopped fresh parsley, plus
  extra to garnish
350 g/12 oz smoked haddock
  fillets, skinned
450 g/1 lb potatoes, cooked
  and mashed
6 tbsp double cream
salt and pepper

TO SERVE
crusty rolls
green salad

serves 4 | *prep* 10 minutes | *cook* 30 minutes

SMOKED COD CHOWDER

25 g/1 oz butter
1 onion, finely chopped
1 small celery stick, finely diced
250 g/9 oz potatoes, diced
55 g/2 oz carrots, diced
300 ml/10 fl oz boiling water
350 g/12 oz smoked cod fillets,
   skinned and cut into
   bite-sized pieces
300 ml/10 fl oz milk
salt and pepper

Melt the butter in a large saucepan over a low heat, add the onion and celery and cook, stirring frequently, for 5 minutes, or until softened but not browned.

Add the potatoes, carrots, water and salt and pepper to taste. Bring to the boil, then reduce the heat and simmer for 10 minutes, or until the vegetables are tender. Add the fish to the chowder and cook for a further 10 minutes.

Pour in the milk and heat gently. Taste and adjust the seasoning, if necessary. Serve hot.

serves 4 | *prep* 20 minutes | *cook* 40–45 minutes

CARIBBEAN FISH CHOWDER

3 tbsp vegetable oil
1 tsp cumin seeds, crushed
1 tsp dried thyme or oregano
1 onion, diced
1/2 green pepper, deseeded and diced
1 sweet potato, diced
2–3 fresh green chillies, deseeded and
  very finely chopped
1 garlic clove, very finely chopped
1 litre/1 3/4 pints chicken stock
400 g/14 oz red snapper fillets,
  skinned and cut into chunks
25 g/1 oz frozen peas
25 g/1 oz frozen sweetcorn kernels
125 ml/4 fl oz single cream
salt and pepper
3 tbsp chopped fresh coriander,
  to garnish

Heat the oil with the cumin seeds and thyme in a large saucepan over a medium heat. Add the onion, pepper, sweet potato, chillies and garlic and cook, stirring constantly, for 1 minute.

Reduce the heat to medium–low, cover and cook for 10 minutes, or until beginning to soften.

Pour in the stock and season generously with salt and pepper. Bring to the boil, then reduce the heat to medium–low, cover and simmer for 20 minutes.

Add the snapper, peas, sweetcorn and cream. Cook over a low heat, uncovered and without boiling, for 7–10 minutes until the fish is just cooked.

Serve immediately, garnished with coriander.

serves 4 | *prep* 10 minutes | *cook* 8–10 minutes

PRAWN LAKSA

Put the coconut milk and stock in a saucepan over a medium heat and bring slowly to the boil. Add all the remaining ingredients, except the prawns, reduce the heat to low and simmer gently for 4–5 minutes until the noodles are cooked.

Add the prawns and simmer for a further 1–2 minutes until heated through. Ladle the soup into small warmed bowls, dividing the prawns equally between them, and serve immediately.

400 g/14 oz canned coconut milk
300 ml/10 fl oz vegetable stock
50 g/1¾ oz dried vermicelli
  rice noodles
1 red pepper, deseeded and cut
  into strips
225 g/8 oz canned bamboo shoots,
  drained and rinsed
5-cm/2-inch piece fresh root ginger,
  thinly sliced
3 spring onions, chopped
1 tbsp Thai Red Curry Paste
2 tbsp Thai fish sauce
1 tsp palm sugar or soft light
  brown sugar
6 fresh Thai basil sprigs
12 cooked prawns, in their shells

serves 4 | *prep* 15 minutes | *cook* 45 minutes

PRAWN GUMBO

Melt the butter with the oil in a large saucepan over a medium heat, add the okra and cook, uncovered and stirring frequently, for 15 minutes, or until the okra loses its gummy consistency.

Add the onion, celery, pepper, garlic, tomatoes, thyme, bay leaf and salt and pepper to taste. Cover and cook over a medium–low heat for 10 minutes.

Pour in the stock. Bring to the boil, then reduce the heat to medium–low, cover and simmer for 15 minutes, or until the vegetables are al dente. Add the prawns and Tabasco sauce and cook for 5 minutes, or until the prawns turn pink.

Stir in the coriander to garnish and serve.

2 tbsp butter
2 tbsp vegetable oil
250 g/9 oz okra, trimmed and
  thickly sliced
1 onion, finely chopped
2 celery sticks, quartered lengthways
  and diced
1 green pepper, deseeded and diced
2 garlic cloves, very finely chopped
200 g/7 oz canned chopped tomatoes
1/2 tsp dried thyme or oregano
1 fresh bay leaf
850 ml/1 1/2 pints chicken stock
  or water
450 g/1 lb fresh or frozen raw prawns,
  peeled and deveined
few drops of Tabasco sauce
salt and pepper
2 tbsp chopped fresh coriander,
  to garnish

serves 4 | *prep* 25 minutes | *cook* 45 minutes

BOUILLABAISSE

100 ml/3¹/₂ fl oz olive oil
3 garlic cloves, chopped
1 onion, chopped
2 spring onions, sliced
2 tomatoes, deseeded and chopped
1 fennel bulb, chopped
700 ml/1¹/₄ pints fish stock
400 ml/14 fl oz dry white wine
1 bay leaf
pinch of saffron threads
1 tbsp chopped fresh oregano
1 tbsp chopped fresh basil
2 tbsp chopped fresh parsley
200 g/7 oz live mussels
500 g/1 lb 2 oz snapper or
  monkfish fillets, skinned
200 g/7 oz cooked prawns, peeled
  and deveined
salt and pepper
thick slices of French bread, to serve

Heat the oil in a large saucepan over a medium heat, add the garlic, onion and spring onions and cook, stirring frequently, for 3 minutes. Stir in the tomatoes, fennel, stock, wine, bay leaf, saffron and herbs. Bring to the boil, then reduce the heat, cover and simmer for 30 minutes.

Meanwhile, clean the mussels by scrubbing or scraping the shells and pulling out any beards that are attached to them. Discard any with broken shells or any that refuse to close when tapped. Put the mussels in a colander and rinse well under cold running water. Put them in a large saucepan with just the water that clings to their shells and cook, covered, over a high heat, shaking the saucepan occasionally, for 3–4 minutes, or until the mussels have opened. Discard any mussels that remain closed. Drain and set aside.

Rinse the snapper under cold running water, pat dry with kitchen paper, then cut into small chunks. Add to the tomato mixture and simmer for 5 minutes. Add the mussels and prawns, season to taste with salt and pepper and cook for 5 minutes, or until the prawns turn pink. Remove and discard the bay leaf and ladle the soup into warmed serving bowls. Serve with thick slices of French bread.

serves 4 | *prep* 25 minutes | *cook* 45 minutes

CIOPPINO

2 tbsp butter
3 tbsp olive oil
2 garlic cloves, chopped
1 onion, chopped
400 g/14 oz canned chopped
   tomatoes
450 ml/16 fl oz fish stock
200 ml/7 fl oz dry white wine
1 bay leaf
1 tsp dried mixed herbs
200 g/7 oz live mussels
350 g/12 oz cod fillets, rinsed, dried
   and cut into chunks
350 g/12 oz raw prawns, peeled
   and deveined
200 g/7 oz cooked lobster meat, cut
   into chunks
salt and pepper
fresh flat-leaf parsley sprigs,
   to garnish
crusty bread, to serve

Melt the butter with the oil in a large saucepan over a medium heat, add the garlic and onion and cook, stirring, for 3 minutes. Stir in the tomatoes, stock, wine, bay leaf and herbs. Bring to the boil, then reduce the heat, cover and simmer for 30 minutes. Meanwhile, clean the mussels by scrubbing or scraping the shells and pulling out any beards that are attached to them. Discard any with broken shells or any that refuse to close when tapped. Put the mussels in a colander and rinse well under cold running water. Put them into a large saucepan with just the water that clings to their shells and cook, covered, over a high heat, shaking the saucepan occasionally, for 3–4 minutes, or until the mussels have opened. Discard any that remain closed. Drain and set aside.

Add the cod to the tomato mixture and simmer for 3 minutes. Add the mussels and prawns and cook for 5 minutes, or until the prawns turn pink. Stir in the lobster, season to taste with salt and pepper and simmer for 1 minute. Remove and discard the bay leaf and ladle the soup into warmed serving bowls. Garnish with parsley sprigs and serve with crusty bread.

serves 4 | *prep* 20 minutes | *cook* 25–30 minutes

NEW ENGLAND CLAM CHOWDER

900 g/2 lb live clams
4 rindless streaky bacon rashers,
  chopped
2 tbsp butter
1 onion, chopped
1 tbsp chopped fresh thyme
1 large potato, diced
300 ml/10 fl oz milk
1 bay leaf
150 ml/5 fl oz double cream
1 tbsp chopped fresh parsley
salt and pepper

Scrub the clams and put in a large saucepan with a splash of water. Cook over a high heat for 3–4 minutes until all the clams have opened. Discard any that remain closed. Drain the clams, reserving the cooking liquid. Set aside until cool enough to handle.

Reserve 8 clams in their shells to garnish. Remove the remaining clams from their shells, roughly chop if large and set aside.

Heat a clean, dry saucepan over a medium–high heat, add the bacon and cook, stirring frequently, for 5 minutes, or until browned and crisp. Remove with a slotted spoon and drain on kitchen paper. Melt the butter in the saucepan, add the onion and cook, stirring frequently, for 4–5 minutes until softened but not browned. Add the thyme and cook briefly before adding the potato, reserved clam cooking liquid, milk and bay leaf. Bring to the boil, then reduce the heat and simmer for 10 minutes, or until the potato is tender but not falling apart.

Leave the soup to cool slightly, then transfer to a blender or food processor and process until smooth.

Return the soup to the saucepan and add the shelled clams, bacon and cream. Simmer for a further 2–3 minutes. Season to taste with salt and pepper and stir in the parsley. Ladle into warmed serving bowls, garnish with the reserved clams in their shells and serve.

serves 4 | *prep* 15 minutes | *cook* 45–50 minutes

BASQUE TUNA STEW

5 tbsp olive oil
1 large onion, chopped
2 garlic cloves, chopped
200 g/7 oz canned chopped
   tomatoes
700 g/1 lb 9 oz potatoes, cut
   into 5-cm/2-inch chunks
3 green peppers, deseeded and
   roughly chopped
300 ml/10 fl oz cold water
900 g/2 lb fresh tuna, cut into
   chunks
4 slices crusty white bread
salt and pepper

Heat 2 tablespoons of the oil in a saucepan over a medium heat, add the onion and cook, stirring frequently, for 8–10 minutes until softened and browned. Add the garlic and cook, stirring, for a further minute. Add the tomatoes, cover and simmer for 30 minutes, or until thickened.

Meanwhile, in a separate saucepan, mix together the potatoes and peppers. Add the water (which should just cover the vegetables) and bring to the boil, then reduce the heat and simmer for 15 minutes, or until the potatoes are almost tender.

Add the tuna and the tomato mixture to the potatoes and peppers and season to taste with salt and pepper. Cover and simmer for 6–8 minutes until the tuna is tender.

Meanwhile, heat the remaining oil in a large frying pan over a medium heat, add the bread slices and fry on both sides until golden. Remove with a slotted spoon and drain on kitchen paper. Serve with the stew.

serves 4 | *prep* 25 minutes | *cook* 55 minutes

CHUNKY COD STEW
WITH CELERY & POTATOES

2 red peppers, halved and deseeded
3 tbsp olive oil
1 onion, finely chopped
2 garlic cloves, very finely chopped
1 tbsp white wine vinegar
1 tbsp tomato purée
1 tbsp dried thyme or oregano
250 ml/9 fl oz fish stock
2 celery sticks, finely sliced
600 g/1 lb 5 oz fresh or frozen thick
   cod steaks, cut into chunks
55 g/2 oz stale coarse white
   breadcrumbs
8–10 black olives, stoned and sliced
salt and pepper
chopped celery leaves, to garnish

Preheat the oven to 200°C/400°F/Gas Mark 6. Cook the peppers, cut-side down, on a baking tray under a preheated hot grill for 10–12 minutes until beginning to blacken. Meanwhile, heat 1 tablespoon of the oil in a flameproof casserole, add the onion and cook, stirring frequently, for 5 minutes. Add the garlic, vinegar, tomato purée and half the thyme. Cook, stirring, for 1 minute. Add the stock and simmer for 5 minutes.

When cool enough to handle, peel the skin off the peppers. Roughly chop the flesh. Put in a blender or food processor with the onion mixture and add salt and pepper to taste. Process until smooth. Pour into the casserole, add the celery and cod and bring to the boil. Cover and bake in the oven for 35 minutes.

Combine the breadcrumbs, remaining oil, olives, remaining thyme and salt and pepper to taste in a small bowl. Sprinkle over the stew. Brown under a hot grill for 5 minutes. Garnish with celery leaves before serving.

serves 4 | *prep* 15 minutes | *cook* 40 minutes

SPANISH SWORDFISH STEW

4 tbsp olive oil
3 shallots, chopped
2 garlic cloves, chopped
225 g/8 oz canned chopped tomatoes
1 tbsp tomato purée
650 g/1 lb 7 oz potatoes, sliced
250 ml/9 fl oz vegetable stock
2 tbsp lemon juice
1 red pepper, deseeded and chopped
1 orange pepper, deseeded
  and chopped
20 black olives, stoned and halved
1 kg/2 lb 4 oz swordfish steak,
  skinned and cut into
  bite-sized pieces
salt and pepper
crusty bread, to serve

TO GARNISH
fresh flat-leaf parsley sprigs
lemon slices

Heat the oil in a saucepan over a low heat, add the shallots and cook, stirring frequently, for 4 minutes, or until softened. Add the garlic, tomatoes and tomato purée, cover and simmer gently for 20 minutes.

Meanwhile, put the potatoes in a flameproof casserole with the stock and lemon juice. Bring to the boil, then reduce the heat and add the peppers. Cover and cook for 15 minutes.

Add the olives, swordfish and the tomato mixture to the potatoes. Season to taste with salt and pepper. Stir well, then cover and simmer for 7–10 minutes, or until the swordfish is cooked to your taste.

Remove from the heat and garnish with parsley sprigs and lemon slices. Serve with crusty bread.

serves 6 | *prep* 20 minutes | *cook* 30 minutes

LOUISIANA GUMBO

2 tbsp sunflower or corn oil
175 g/6 oz okra, trimmed and cut into
  2.5-cm/1-inch pieces
2 onions, very finely chopped
4 celery sticks, very finely chopped
1 garlic clove, finely chopped
2 tbsp plain flour
1/2 tsp sugar
1 tsp ground cumin
700 ml/1 1/4 pints fish stock
1 red pepper, deseeded and chopped
1 green pepper, deseeded
  and chopped
2 large tomatoes
350 g/12 oz large raw prawns
4 tbsp chopped fresh parsley
1 tbsp chopped fresh coriander
dash of Tabasco sauce, or to taste
350 g/12 oz cod or haddock
  fillets, skinned and cut into
  2.5-cm/1-inch cubes
350 g/12 oz monkfish fillets, cut
  into 2.5-cm/1-inch cubes
salt and pepper

Heat half the oil in a large, flameproof casserole over a low heat, add the okra and cook, stirring frequently, for 5 minutes, or until browned. Remove with a slotted spoon and set aside. Heat the remaining oil in the casserole, add the onion and celery and cook, stirring frequently, for 5 minutes, or until softened. Add the garlic and cook, stirring, for 1 minute. Stir in the flour, sugar, cumin and salt and pepper to taste. Cook, stirring, for 2 minutes, then gradually stir in the stock and bring to the boil, stirring constantly.

Return the reserved okra to the casserole and add the peppers and tomatoes. Partially cover, reduce the heat to very low and simmer gently, stirring occasionally, for 10 minutes. Peel and devein the prawns and set aside.

Add the parsley, coriander and Tabasco sauce to the casserole, then gently stir in the fish and prawns. Cover and simmer gently for 5 minutes, or until the fish is cooked through and the prawns turn pink. Transfer to a large, warmed serving dish and serve.

serves 4–6 | *prep* 35 minutes | *cook* 30–35 minutes

CATALAN FISH STEW

large pinch of saffron threads
4 tbsp boiling water
6 tbsp olive oil
1 large onion, chopped
2 garlic cloves, finely chopped
1½ tbsp chopped fresh thyme leaves
2 bay leaves
2 red peppers, deseeded and
   roughly chopped
800 g/1 lb 12 oz canned chopped
   tomatoes
1 tsp smoked paprika
250 ml/9 fl oz fish stock
140 g/5 oz blanched almonds, toasted
   and finely ground
600 g/1 lb 5 oz thick hake or cod
   fillets, skinned and cut into 5-cm/
   2-inch chunks
12–16 raw prawns, peeled and
   deveined
12–16 live mussels, scrubbed and
   debearded
12–16 live clams, scrubbed
salt and pepper
thick crusty bread, to serve

Stir in the stock, reserved saffron water and ground almonds and bring to the boil, stirring frequently. Reduce the heat and simmer for 5–10 minutes until the sauce reduces and thickens. Add salt and pepper to taste.

Gently stir in the hake so that it doesn't break up and add the prawns, mussels and clams. Reduce the heat to very low, cover the casserole and simmer for 5 minutes, or until the hake is cooked through, the prawns turn pink and the mussels and clams open; discard any mussels or clams that remain closed. Serve immediately with plenty of thick, crusty bread for soaking up the juices.

Put the saffron threads in a heatproof bowl, add the boiling water and set aside to infuse.

Heat the oil in a large, heavy-based, flameproof casserole over a medium–high heat. Reduce the heat to low, add the onion and cook, stirring occasionally, for 10 minutes, or until golden but not browned. Stir in the garlic, thyme, bay leaves and peppers and cook for 5 minutes, or until the peppers are soft .

Add the tomatoes and paprika and simmer, stirring frequently, for 5 minutes.

serves 4 | *prep* 30 minutes | *cook* 25 minutes

BRAZILIAN SEAFOOD STEW

2 tbsp olive oil
1 onion, finely chopped
2 garlic cloves, very finely chopped
400 g/14 oz canned
  chopped tomatoes
1/4 tsp cayenne pepper
pinch of saffron threads
900 g/2 lb cod steaks, cut into chunks
450 g/1 lb mussels, scrubbed
  and debearded
225 g/8 oz raw tiger prawns, peeled
  and deveined
200 g/7 oz canned crabmeat, drained
200 g/7 oz bottled clams
salt and pepper
3 tbsp chopped fresh coriander,
  to garnish

Heat the oil in a large saucepan or flameproof casserole over a medium heat, add the onion and cook, stirring frequently, for 5 minutes, or until softened.

Stir in the garlic, tomatoes, cayenne pepper and saffron. Season to taste with salt and pepper and simmer, stirring occasionally, for 5 minutes.

Add the cod and mussels, then pour in enough water to just cover and bring to the boil. Reduce the heat to low, cover and simmer for 10 minutes, or until the mussels have opened. Discard any that remain closed.

Add the prawns, crabmeat and clams with their juice. Simmer for a further 5 minutes, or until the prawns turn pink.

Stir in the coriander just before serving.

5

Enjoy fish at its laid-back, comforting best in this selection of classic dishes. Here it is combined with eggs, simmered with rice, tossed with pasta and noodles or encased in rich, crumbling pastry or a crisp breadcrumb or batter coating. It is even wrapped up in a warm tortilla for good measure.

LIGHT LUNCHES AND SUPPER DISHES

While fresh fish features in many of the recipes – including smoked fish, which works so well with cheese and spices – several dishes use storecupboard or freezer ingredients for convenience. Canned anchovies, for instance, along with bottled olives and capers, make a gutsy impromptu pasta sauce, and frozen prawns and canned tuna combine to create a tasty seafood omelette.

serves 4 | *prep* 10 minutes | *cook* 30 minutes

KEDGEREE

450 g/1 lb undyed smoked haddock, skinned
2 tbsp olive oil
1 onion, finely chopped
1 tsp mild curry paste
175 g/6 oz long-grain white rice
55 g/2 oz butter
3 hard-boiled eggs
salt and pepper
2 tbsp chopped fresh parsley, to garnish

Put the fish in a large saucepan and cover with water. Bring the water to the boil, then reduce the heat and simmer for 8–10 minutes until the fish flakes easily.

Remove the fish with a slotted spoon and keep warm, reserving the cooking liquid in a jug or bowl.

Heat the oil in the saucepan over a medium heat, add the onion and cook, stirring frequently, for 4 minutes, or until softened. Stir in the curry paste and add the rice.

Measure 600 ml/1 pint of the haddock cooking liquid and return to the saucepan. Bring to a simmer and cover. Cook for 10–12 minutes until the rice is tender and the water has been absorbed. Season to taste with salt and pepper.

Flake the fish and add to the saucepan with the butter. Stir very gently over a low heat until the butter has melted. Chop 2 of the hard-boiled eggs and add to the saucepan.

Turn the kedgeree into a serving dish, slice the remaining egg and use to garnish. Scatter over the chopped parsley and serve immediately.

serves 6 | *prep 25 minutes, plus 40 minutes' chilling and resting* | *cook 30 minutes*

SMOKED HADDOCK & GRUYERE SOUFFLE TART

PASTRY
125 g/4^{1}/$_2$ oz plain flour, plus extra
  for dusting
pinch of salt
75 g/2^{3}/$_4$ oz cold butter, diced, plus
  extra for greasing
^{1}/$_2$ tsp English mustard powder
1 egg yolk

FILLING
250 g/9 oz undyed smoked haddock
300 ml/10 fl oz milk
1 bay leaf
25 g/1 oz butter
25 g/1 oz plain flour
^{1}/$_2$ tsp ground nutmeg
125 g/4^{1}/$_2$ oz Gruyère cheese, grated
2 eggs, separated
white pepper

Lightly grease a 23-cm/9-inch loose-based fluted tart tin. Sift the flour with the salt into a food processor, add the butter and process until the mixture resembles fine breadcrumbs. Tip the mixture into a large bowl and sprinkle in the mustard powder. Mix the egg yolk with a little cold water and add a little of the mixture to the bowl, just enough to bring the dough together. Turn out onto a lightly floured work surface and roll out the pastry to a circle 8 cm/3^{1}/$_4$ inches wider in diameter than the tin. Line the tin with the pastry and trim the edge. Line the tart case with baking paper and fill with baking beans. Chill in the refrigerator for 30 minutes. Meanwhile, preheat the oven to 190°C/375°F/Gas Mark 5.

Remove the tart case from the refrigerator and bake in the preheated oven for 10 minutes. Remove the paper and beans and bake the tart case for a further 5 minutes.

Meanwhile, put the milk and bay leaf in a frying pan and bring to a simmer. Add the haddock and cook for 3–5 minutes until just cooked. Remove and discard the bay leaf and carefully remove the fish with a slotted spoon, reserving the milk. When cool enough to handle, flake the fish, removing and discarding any bones or skin. Increase the oven temperature to 200°C/400°F/Gas Mark 6.

Melt the butter in a saucepan, stir in the flour and cook, stirring constantly, for 2–3 minutes. Gradually add the reserved cooking milk and cook, stirring constantly, for another 5 minutes, or until thickened. Stir in the nutmeg and pepper to taste, then the cheese. Remove the sauce from the heat, stir in the egg yolks and fish and leave to cool slightly. Meanwhile, whisk the egg whites in a clean, grease-free bowl until stiff, then fold quickly and lightly into the fish mixture. Immediately pour into the tart case and bake for 15 minutes until puffed up and browned. Remove the tart from the oven, leave to rest for 10 minutes, then serve.

serves 2 | *prep* 10 minutes | *cook* 20 minutes

OMELETTE ARNOLD BENNETT

175 g/6 oz undyed smoked haddock,
  skinned
25 g/1 oz butter
4 eggs
1 tbsp olive oil
4 tbsp single cream
2 tbsp grated Cheddar or
  Parmesan cheese
salt and pepper

Put the haddock in a large saucepan and cover with water. Bring the water to the boil, then reduce the heat and simmer for 8–10 minutes until the fish flakes easily. Remove the fish with a slotted spoon and drain onto a plate. When cool enough to handle, flake the fish, removing and discarding any bones.

Melt half the butter in a small saucepan and add the haddock to warm.

In a bowl, beat the eggs together gently with a fork and season to taste with salt and pepper, taking care not to add too much salt because the haddock will be quite salty.

Melt the remaining butter with the oil in a 23-cm/9-inch frying pan with a heatproof handle over a medium heat. When the butter starts to froth, pour in the eggs and spread them around by tilting the frying pan. Use a spatula or fork to move the egg around until it is cooked underneath but still liquid on top.

Tip in the warm haddock and spread over the omelette.

Pour over the cream and top with the cheese, then place the frying pan under a preheated hot grill for 1 minute until the cheese is melted. Serve immediately on warmed plates.

serves 4 | *prep* 30 minutes, plus 30 minutes' chilling | *cook* 15–20 minutes

HADDOCK GOUJONS

175 g/6 oz herb focaccia bread
700 g/1 lb 9 oz skinless, boneless
  haddock fillet
2–3 tbsp plain flour
2 eggs, lightly beaten
vegetable oil, for deep-frying
fresh parsley sprigs, to garnish
lemon wedges, to serve

TARTARE SAUCE
1 egg yolk
1 tsp Dijon mustard
2 tsp white wine vinegar
150 ml/5 fl oz light olive oil
1 tsp finely chopped green olives
1 tsp finely chopped gherkins
1 tsp finely chopped capers
2 tsp snipped fresh chives
2 tsp chopped fresh parsley
salt and pepper

Put the focaccia in a food processor and process to fine breadcrumbs. Set aside. Thinly slice the haddock fillet widthways into fingers. Put the flour, egg and breadcrumbs in separate bowls.

Dip the haddock fingers into the flour, then the egg and finally the breadcrumbs to coat. Lay on a plate, cover and chill in the refrigerator for 30 minutes. To make the tartare sauce, put the egg yolk, mustard, vinegar and salt and pepper to taste in a blender or clean food processor. Process for 30 seconds until frothy. Begin adding the olive oil through the feed tube, drop by drop, until the mixture begins to thicken. Continue adding the oil in a slow, steady stream until all the oil is incorporated.

Transfer to a small bowl and stir in the remaining ingredients. Check and adjust the seasoning, if necessary. Add a little hot water if the sauce is too thick.

Heat the vegetable oil in deep-fat fryer, large, heavy-based saucepan or wok to 180–190°C/ 350–375°F, or until a cube of bread browns in 30 seconds. Fry 3–4 goujons at a time for 3–4 minutes until the crumbs are browned and crisp and the fish is cooked. Remove with a slotted spoon and drain on kitchen paper. Keep warm while you cook the remaining fish.

Serve the goujons immediately, with tartare sauce and lemon wedges for squeezing over.

serves 6 | *prep* 20 minutes | *cook* 40 minutes

SALMON FRITTATA

250 g/9 oz skinless, boneless salmon
3 fresh thyme sprigs
1 fresh parsley sprig plus 2 tbsp
  chopped fresh parsley
5 black peppercorns
1/2 small onion, sliced
1/2 stick celery, sliced
1/2 carrot, chopped
175 g/6 oz asparagus spears, chopped
85 g/3 oz baby carrots, halved
50 g/1 3/4 oz butter
1 large onion, finely sliced
1 garlic clove, finely chopped
115 g/4 oz fresh or frozen peas
8 eggs, lightly beaten
1 tbsp chopped fresh dill
salt and pepper
lemon wedges, to garnish

TO SERVE
crème fraîche
salad
crusty bread

Put the salmon in a saucepan with 1 thyme sprig, the parsley sprig, peppercorns, onion, celery and carrot. Cover the vegetables and fish with cold water and bring slowly to the boil. Remove the saucepan from the heat and leave to stand for 5 minutes. Remove the fish with a slotted spoon, flake and set aside. Discard the vegetables and cooking liquid.

Bring a large saucepan of salted water to the boil and blanch the asparagus for 2 minutes. Drain and refresh under cold running water. Blanch the baby carrots for 4 minutes. Drain and refresh under cold running water. Drain both again and pat dry. Set aside.

Heat half the butter in a large frying pan with a flameproof handle over a medium–low heat, add the onion and cook, stirring occasionally, for 8–10 minutes until softened but not browned. Add the garlic and remaining thyme and cook, stirring, for a further minute. Add the asparagus, carrot and peas and heat through.

Transfer to the eggs in a bowl with the chopped parsley, dill, salmon and salt and pepper to taste. Stir briefly. Heat the remaining butter in the pan over a low heat and return the mixture to the pan. Cover and cook for 10 minutes.

Cook under a preheated medium grill for a further 5 minutes until set and golden. Serve hot or cold in wedges, topped with a dollop of crème fraîche, with salad and crusty bread. Garnish with lemon wedges.

serves 3 | *prep* 20 minutes | *cook* 25 minutes

SEAFOOD OMELETTE

25 g/1 oz unsalted butter
1 tbsp olive oil
1 onion, very finely chopped
175 g/6 oz courgettes, halved
  lengthways and sliced
1 celery stick, very finely chopped
85 g/3 oz button mushrooms, sliced
55 g/2 oz French beans, cut into
  5-cm/2-inch lengths
4 eggs
85 g/3 oz mascarpone cheese
1 tbsp chopped fresh thyme
1 tbsp shredded fresh basil
200 g/7 oz canned tuna, drained
  and flaked
115 g/4 oz cooked peeled prawns,
  thawed if frozen
salt and pepper

Melt the butter with the oil in a heavy-based frying pan with a flameproof handle over a low heat. Add the onion and cook, stirring occasionally, for 5 minutes until softened.

Add the courgettes, celery, mushrooms and beans and cook, stirring occasionally, for a further 8–10 minutes until beginning to brown.

Beat the eggs with the cheese, thyme, basil and salt and pepper to taste in a bowl.

Add the tuna to the frying pan and stir it into the mixture with a wooden spoon, then stir in the prawns.

Pour the egg mixture into the frying pan and cook for 5 minutes, or until it is just beginning to set. Draw the egg from the sides of the frying pan towards the centre to allow the uncooked egg to run underneath.

Put the frying pan under a preheated hot grill and cook until the egg is set and the surface is beginning to brown. Cut the omelette into wedges and serve.

serves 4 | *prep* 15 minutes, plus 5 hours' chilling | *cook* 12 minutes

PAN BAGNA

40-cm/16-inch country-style loaf,
   thicker than a French baguette
fruity extra virgin olive oil
ready-made tapenade (optional)

FILLING
2 eggs
50 g/1³/4 oz canned anchovy fillets
   in oil
about 85 g/3 oz herb-, garlic- or chilli-
   flavoured olives
lettuce or rocket leaves, rinsed and
   patted dry
about 4 plum tomatoes, sliced
200 g/7 oz canned tuna in brine, well
   drained and flaked

Bring a saucepan of water to the boil, add the eggs and return to the boil. Boil for 12 minutes. Drain and immediately plunge into a bowl of ice-cold water to prevent further cooking.

Shell the cooked eggs and cut into slices. Drain the anchovy fillets well, then cut them in half lengthways if large. Stone the olives and halve. Set aside.

Using a serrated knife, slice the loaf horizontally in half. Remove about 1 cm/ ¹/2 inch of the crumb from the top and bottom, leaving a border all around both halves.

Generously brush both halves with the oil. Spread with tapenade, if you like a strong, robust flavour. Arrange a layer of lettuce leaves on the bottom half.

Add layers of hard-boiled egg slices, tomato slices, olives, anchovies and tuna, sprinkling with oil and adding lettuce leaves between the layers. Make the filling as thick as you like.

Place the other bread half on top and press down firmly. Wrap tightly in clingfilm and put on a board or plate that will fit in your refrigerator. Weight down with food cans and chill in the refrigerator for several hours. To serve, slice into 4 equal portions, tying with string to secure in place, if wished.

serves 4 | *prep* 20 minutes, plus 30 minutes' chilling | *cook* 30–35 minutes

FISH CAKES

450 g/1 lb floury potatoes, such as
   King Edward, Maris Piper or Desirée,
   peeled and cut into chunks
450 g/1 lb mixed fish fillets, such as
   cod and salmon, skinned
2 tbsp chopped fresh tarragon
grated rind of 1 lemon
2 tbsp double cream
1 tbsp plain flour
1 egg, beaten
115 g/4 oz breadcrumbs, made from
   day-old white or wholemeal bread
4 tbsp vegetable oil
salt and pepper
lemon wedges, to garnish
watercress salad, to serve

Bring a large saucepan of salted water
to the boil, add the potatoes and cook for
15–20 minutes. Drain well, then mash with a
potato masher or fork until smooth.

Put the fish in a frying pan and just cover with
water. Bring to the boil over a medium heat,
then reduce the heat to low, cover and
simmer gently for 5 minutes until cooked.

Remove with a slotted spoon and drain on a
plate. When cool enough to handle, flake the
fish roughly into good-sized pieces, removing
and discarding any bones.

Mix the mashed potatoes with the fish,
tarragon, lemon rind and cream in a bowl.
Season well with salt and pepper and shape
into 4 round cakes or 8 smaller ones with
your hands.

Put the flour, egg and breadcrumbs in
separate bowls. Dust the fish cakes with flour,
dip into the beaten egg, then coat thoroughly
in the breadcrumbs. Put on a baking tray,
cover and chill in the refrigerator for at least
30 minutes.

Heat the oil in the frying pan over a medium
heat, add the fish cakes and cook for
5 minutes on each side, turning them carefully
using a palette knife or a fish slice.

Serve hot with a watercress salad.

serves 4 | *prep* 25 minutes, plus 30 minutes' resting | *cook* 20 minutes

DEEP-FRIED SEAFOOD

corn oil, for deep-frying
200 g/7 oz white fish fillets, such as
   lemon sole, skinned and cut
   into strips
200 g/7 oz monkfish fillets, cut into
   bite-sized chunks
4 live scallops, shucked and cleaned
225 g/8 oz large cooked prawns,
   peeled and deveined but
   with tails left intact

BATTER
115 g/4 oz plain flour
pinch of salt
1 egg yolk
1 tbsp olive oil
225 ml/8 fl oz milk
2 egg whites

TO GARNISH
fresh flat-leaf parsley sprigs
lemon wedges

First, make the batter. Sift the flour with the salt into a bowl and make a well in the centre. Add the egg yolk and olive oil to the well and mix together with a wooden spoon, gradually incorporating the flour. Gradually beat in the milk to make a smooth batter. Cover and leave to rest for 30 minutes.

Heat the corn oil in a deep-fat fryer, large, heavy-based saucepan or wok to 180–190°C/ 350–375°F, or until a cube of bread browns in 30 seconds.

Meanwhile, whisk the egg whites in a separate clean, grease-free bowl until they form stiff peaks. Gently fold into the batter.

Using tongs, dip the seafood, a piece at a time, into the batter to coat. Fry in small batches for 3–4 minutes until crisp and golden (if you fry too many pieces at a time, the oil temperature will drop and the batter will be soggy). Remove with a slotted spoon and drain on kitchen paper. Transfer to a warmed serving platter and keep warm in a low oven while you cook the remaining pieces.

Garnish with parsley sprigs and lemon wedges and serve.

serves 4 | *prep* 15 minutes | *cook* 20–25 minutes

FISH TACOS

¼ red cabbage, thinly sliced
  or shredded
¼ tsp dried oregano
¼ tsp ground cumin
1 tsp mild chilli powder
2 garlic cloves, finely chopped
juice of 2 limes
hot pepper sauce or salsa, to taste
about 450 g/1 lb firm-fleshed white
  fish fillets, such as red snapper or
  cod, skinned and cut into chunks
3 tbsp plain flour
vegetable oil, for frying
8 corn tortillas
1 tbsp chopped fresh coriander
½ onion, chopped (optional)
salsa of your choice
salt and pepper

Combine the cabbage with half the oregano, cumin, chilli powder and garlic, then stir in the lime juice and salt and hot pepper sauce to taste. Set aside.

Put the fish on a plate and sprinkle with the remaining oregano, cumin, chilli powder and garlic and salt and pepper to taste. Dust with the flour.

Heat the oil in a frying pan over a high heat until it is smoking, add the fish and fry, turning frequently, in small batches until golden on the outside and just tender in the centre. Remove with a slotted spoon and drain on kitchen paper. Keep warm in a low oven while you cook the remaining fish.

Heat the tortillas one by one in a dry non-stick frying pan over a medium heat, sprinkling with a few drops of water as they heat; wrap the tortillas in a clean tea towel as you work to keep them warm. Alternatively, heat through in a stack in the pan, alternating the tortillas from the top to the bottom to warm evenly.

Put some of the warm fried fish in each tortilla, along with a large spoonful of the hot cabbage salad. Sprinkle with chopped fresh coriander and onion, if desired. Add the salsa to taste and serve immediately.

serves 4 | *prep* 15 minutes, plus 15 minutes' cooling | *cook* 15–20 minutes

FISH & REFRIED BEAN TOSTADAS

about 450 g/1 lb firm-fleshed white fish
    fillets, such as red snapper or cod,
    skinned
125 ml/4 fl oz fish stock
1/4 tsp ground cumin
1/4 tsp mild chilli powder
pinch of dried oregano
4 garlic cloves, finely chopped
juice of 1/2 lemon or lime
8 soft corn tortillas
vegetable oil, for frying
400 g/14 oz canned refried beans,
    warmed with 2 tbsp water to thin
salsa of your choice
2–3 cos lettuce leaves, shredded
3 tbsp chopped fresh coriander
2 tbsp chopped onion
salt and pepper

TO GARNISH
soured cream
chopped fresh herbs

Put the fish in a saucepan with the stock, cumin, chilli powder, oregano, garlic and salt and pepper to taste. Bring to the boil over a medium heat, then immediately remove from the heat and leave the fish to cool in the cooking liquid.

When cool enough to handle, remove the fish with a slotted spoon, reserving the cooking liquid. Flake the fish into bite-sized pieces and put in a non-metallic bowl. Sprinkle with the lemon juice and set aside.

Heat a little oil in a non-stick frying pan over a high heat, add a tortilla and fry on both sides until crisp. Drain on kitchen paper and keep warm while you cook the remainder. Spread the tostadas with the warm refried beans.

Gently reheat the fish with a little of the reserved fish cooking liquid in a saucepan. Spoon on top of the beans. Top each tostada with some salsa, lettuce, coriander and onion. Garnish each with a dollop of soured cream and a sprinkling of herbs. Serve at once.

serves 4–6 | *prep* 10 minutes, plus 30 minutes' cooling | *cook* 10 minutes

FISH BURRITOS

about 450 g/1 lb firm-fleshed white
  fish fillets, such as red snapper
  or cod, skinned
1/4 tsp ground cumin
pinch of dried oregano
4 garlic cloves, finely chopped
125 ml/4 fl oz fish stock
juice of 1/2 lemon or lime
8 flour tortillas
2–3 cos lettuce leaves, shredded
2 ripe tomatoes, diced
salsa of your choice
salt and pepper
lemon slices, to garnish

Season the fish to taste with salt and pepper, then put in a saucepan with the cumin, oregano, garlic and enough stock to cover.

Bring to the boil and boil for 1 minute. Remove the saucepan from the heat and leave the fish to cool in the cooking liquid for about 30 minutes.

Remove the fish with a slotted spoon. Flake the fish into bite-sized pieces and put in a non-metallic bowl. Sprinkle with the lemon juice and set aside.

Heat the tortillas in a dry non-stick frying pan over a medium heat, sprinkling with a few drops of water as they heat; wrap in a clean tea towel as you work to keep them warm. Alternatively, heat through in a stack in the pan, alternating the tortillas from the top to the bottom to warm evenly.

Arrange some lettuce in the centre of 1 tortilla, spoon on a few fish chunks, then sprinkle with a little tomato. Top with some salsa. Repeat with the other tortillas and serve immediately, garnished with lemon slices.

serves 4 | *prep* 15 minutes, plus 30 minutes' chilling | *cook* 15 minutes

FISH & YOGURT QUENELLES

750 g/1 lb 10 oz white fish fillets, such
   as cod, coley or whiting, skinned
2 small egg whites
1/2 tsp ground coriander
1 tsp ground mace
150 ml/5 fl oz low-fat natural yogurt
1 small onion, sliced
salt and pepper
mixed boiled basmati and wild rice,
   to serve

SAUCE
1 bunch of watercress
300 ml/10 fl oz chicken stock
2 tbsp cornflour
150 ml/5 fl oz low-fat natural yogurt
2 tbsp low-fat crème fraîche

Cut the fish into pieces, put in a food processor and process for about 30 seconds. Add the egg whites and process for a further 30 seconds until the mixture forms a stiff paste. Add the coriander, mace, yogurt and salt and pepper to taste and process until smooth. Transfer to a bowl, cover and chill in the refrigerator for at least 30 minutes.

Spoon the mixture into a piping bag and pipe into sausage shapes about 10 cm/ 4 inches long. Alternatively, take rounded dessertspoons of the mixture and shape into ovals using 2 spoons.

Bring about 5 cm/2 inches of water to the boil in a frying pan and add the onion. Using a fish slice or spoon, lower the quenelles into the water. Cover and gently boil the quenelles for 8 minutes, turning once. Remove with a slotted spoon and drain.

To make the sauce, roughly chop the watercress, reserving a few sprigs for garnishing. Put into a blender or food processor with the stock and process until well blended. Pour into a small saucepan. Stir the cornflour into the yogurt and pour the mixture into the saucepan. Bring to the boil, stirring constantly.

Stir in the crème fraîche and salt and pepper to taste, then remove from the heat. Garnish with the watercress sprigs. Serve with rice.

serves 4 | *prep* 10 minutes | *cook* 20–30 minutes

FRESH SARDINES BAKED
WITH LEMON & OREGANO

2 lemons, plus extra lemon wedges,
  to garnish
12 large fresh sardines, cleaned
4 tbsp olive oil
4 tbsp chopped fresh oregano
salt and pepper

Preheat the oven to 190°C/375°F/Gas Mark 5. Slice 1 of the lemons and grate the rind and squeeze the juice from the second lemon.

Cut the heads off the sardines. Put the fish in a shallow, ovenproof dish large enough to hold them in a single layer. Put the lemon slices between the fish. Drizzle the lemon juice and oil over the fish. Sprinkle over the lemon rind and oregano and season to taste with salt and pepper.

Bake in the preheated oven for 20–30 minutes until the fish are tender. Serve garnished with lemon wedges.

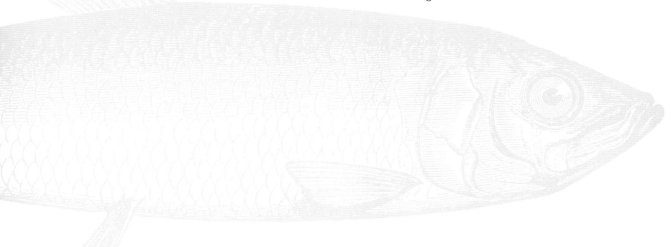

serves 6–8 | prep 20 minutes, plus 1 hour 40 minutes' chilling and resting | cook 1 hour 40 minutes

PISSALADIERE

about 6 tbsp olive oil
3 large garlic cloves, crushed
1 kg/2 lb 4 oz onions, thinly sliced
3–4 tbsp ready-made tapenade
50 g/1¾ oz canned anchovy fillets in
   oil, drained and halved lengthways
12 black olives, stoned
finely chopped fresh flat-leaf parsley,
   to garnish

PASTRY
175 g/6 oz plain flour
pinch of salt
85 g/3 oz butter, diced
2–3 tbsp ice-cold water

To make the pastry, sift the flour with the salt into a bowl. Rub the butter into the flour until fine crumbs form. Mix in 2 tablespoons of the water to make a dough. Only add the extra water if necessary. Lightly knead the dough, then shape into a ball, wrap in clingfilm and chill in the refrigerator for at least 1 hour.

Heat the oil in a large frying pan with a tight-fitting lid over a medium heat, add the garlic and cook, stirring, for 2 minutes. Add the onions and stir to coat in oil. Reduce the heat to its lowest setting.

Dip a piece of baking paper, large enough to fit over the top of the pan, in water. Shake off the excess and press it onto the onions. Cover with the lid and cook for 45 minutes, or until tender.

Meanwhile, roll out the dough on a lightly floured work surface and use to line a 20-cm/8-inch loose-based tart tin. Prick all over with a fork, line with baking paper and fill with baking beans. Chill in the refrigerator for 30 minutes. Preheat the oven to 220°C/425°F/Gas Mark 7.

Put the pastry case on a preheated baking tray and bake for 15 minutes. Remove the paper and beans and bake for a further 5 minutes. Reduce the oven temperature to 180°C/350°F/Gas Mark 4.

Spread the tapenade over the baked pastry case, then fill with the onions. Arrange the anchovy fillets in a lattice pattern and scatter over the olives.

Bake for 25–30 minutes. Leave to rest for 10 minutes. Remove from the tin, scatter with parsley and serve.

serves 4 | *prep* 10 minutes | *cook* 30 minutes

LINGUINE WITH ANCHOVIES, OLIVES & CAPERS

3 tbsp olive oil
2 garlic cloves, finely chopped
10 canned anchovy fillets in oil, drained and chopped
140 g/5 oz black olives, stoned and chopped
1 tbsp capers, rinsed
450 g/1 lb plum tomatoes, peeled, deseeded and chopped
pinch of cayenne pepper
400 g/14 oz dried linguine
salt
2 tbsp chopped fresh flat-leaf parsley, to garnish

Heat the oil in a heavy-based saucepan over a low heat, add the garlic and cook, stirring frequently, for 2 minutes. Add the anchovies and mash them to a pulp with a fork. Add the olives, capers and tomatoes and season to taste with cayenne pepper. Cover and simmer for 25 minutes.

Meanwhile, bring a saucepan of lightly salted water to the boil. Add the pasta, return to the boil and cook for 8–10 minutes until tender but still firm to the bite. Drain the pasta and transfer to a warmed serving dish.

Spoon the anchovy sauce into the dish and toss the pasta using 2 large forks. Garnish with chopped parsley and serve immediately.

serves 6 | *prep* 15 minutes | *cook* 15 minutes

CREAMY SMOKED TROUT TAGLIATELLE

2 carrots, cut into thin batons
2 celery sticks, cut into thin batons
1 courgette, cut into thin batons
1 leek, cut into thin batons
115 g/4 oz fresh or frozen peas
150 ml/5 fl oz vegetable stock
225 g/8 oz smoked trout fillets,
  skinned and cut into thin strips
200 g/7 oz cream cheese
150 ml/5 fl oz dry white wine
2 tbsp chopped fresh dill, plus extra
  sprigs to garnish
225 g/8 oz dried tagliatelle
salt and pepper

Put the carrots, celery, courgette, leek and peas in a large, heavy-based saucepan and pour in the stock. Bring to the boil, then reduce the heat and simmer for 5 minutes, or until the vegetables are tender and most of the stock has evaporated. Remove the saucepan from the heat, stir in the smoked trout and cover to keep warm.

Put the cheese and wine in a separate large, heavy-based saucepan over a low heat and stir until the cheese has melted and the mixture is smooth. Stir in the chopped dill and season to taste with salt and pepper.

Meanwhile, bring another large, heavy-based saucepan of lightly salted water to the boil. Add the pasta, return to the boil and cook for 8–10 minutes until tender but still firm to the bite. Drain the pasta and tip into the cheese sauce. Toss the pasta using 2 large forks, then transfer to a warmed serving dish. Top with the smoked trout mixture, garnish with dill sprigs and serve immediately.

serves 4 | *prep* 15 minutes, plus 20 minutes' soaking | *cook* 10 minutes

SINGAPORE NOODLES

200 g/7 oz dried rice vermicelli
   noodles
1 tbsp mild, medium or hot curry
   paste, to taste
1 tsp turmeric
6 tbsp water
2 tbsp groundnut or sunflower oil
½ onion, very thinly sliced
2 large garlic cloves, thinly sliced
85 g/3 oz broccoli, cut into
   very small florets
85 g/3 oz French beans, cut into
   2.5-cm/1-inch pieces
85 g/3 oz pork fillet, cut in half
   lengthways and then into thin strips,
   or skinless, boneless chicken breast,
   thinly sliced
85 g/3 oz small cooked peeled
   prawns, thawed if frozen
55 g/2 oz Chinese leaves or cos
   lettuce, thinly shredded
¼ fresh bird's-eye chilli, or
   to taste, deseeded and thinly sliced
2 spring onions, light green parts only,
   thinly shredded
fresh coriander, to garnish

Soak the noodles in enough lukewarm water to cover in a bowl for 20 minutes, or until soft. Alternatively, cook according to the packet instructions. Drain and set aside until required. Meanwhile, put the curry paste and turmeric in a small bowl and stir in 4 tablespoons of the water, then set aside.

Heat a wok or large frying pan over a high heat, add the oil and heat until it simmers. Add the onion and garlic and stir-fry for 1 minute, or until softened. Add the broccoli and beans to the wok with the remaining water and stir-fry for a further 2 minutes. Add the pork and stir-fry for 1 minute. Add the prawns, Chinese leaves and chilli to the wok and stir-fry for a further 2 minutes, or until the meat is cooked through and the vegetables are tender but still have a little bite. Remove with a slotted spoon and keep warm.

Add the spring onions, noodles and curry paste mixture to the wok. Mix the noodles and onions together using 2 forks and stir-fry for a further 2 minutes, or until the noodles are hot and have picked up a dark golden colour from the turmeric. Return the other ingredients to the wok and continue stir-frying and mixing for a further minute. Serve immediately, garnished with fresh coriander.

serves 4 | *prep* 15 minutes, plus 20 minutes' soaking | *cook* 10 minutes

PAD THAI

200 g/7 oz dried medium or thick rice
noodles
2 tbsp soft light brown sugar
1 tbsp tamarind paste or 2 tbsp
lemon juice
1 tbsp hot water
4 tbsp salted peanuts
1 tbsp groundnut or sunflower oil
1 shallot, finely chopped
300 g/10 1/2 oz small cooked peeled
prawns, thawed if frozen
2 large eggs, beaten
55 g/2 oz firm tofu (drained weight),
crumbled
2 tbsp Thai fish sauce
1 spring onion, finely chopped
50 g/1 3/4 oz beansprouts
large pinch of white sugar
pinch of dried chilli flakes, or to taste
chopped fresh coriander, to garnish

Soak the noodles in enough lukewarm water
to cover in a bowl for 20 minutes, or until soft.
Alternatively, cook according to the packet
instructions. Drain well and set aside.
Meanwhile, mix the brown sugar, tamarind paste
and hot water together in a separate bowl,
stirring until the tamarind dissolves. Set aside.

Heat a wok or large frying pan over a high heat,
add the peanuts and dry-fry, stirring constantly,
until they just turn golden. Immediately tip the
peanuts out of the wok, then finely chop and
set aside.

When you are ready to start cooking, reheat the
wok over a high heat, add the oil and heat until
it shimmers. Add the shallot and stir-fry for
30 seconds–1 minute until it starts to colour.
Add the prawns and stir-fry for a further
30 seconds. Reduce the heat to medium. Push
the shallot and prawns to one side of the wok,
pour the eggs into the wok and stir-fry until they
are scrambled and firmly set. (You don't want
softly scrambled breakfast eggs for this.)

Return the heat to high, add the tofu to the pan
and stir-fry to colour. Add the noodles, tamarind
mixture, fish sauce, spring onion, beansprouts,
white sugar and chilli flakes. Mix all the
ingredients together using 2 large forks and
stir-fry for a further 2 minutes to warm through.
Serve immediately, sprinkled with coriander.

serves 2 | *prep* 15 minutes, plus 10 minutes' standing | *cook* 20–25 minutes

SEAFOOD PIZZA

1 packet pizza dough mix, about 140 g/5 oz
plain flour, for dusting
extra virgin olive oil, for oiling and drizzling
3–4 tbsp ready-made tomato pasta sauce
225 g/8 oz mixed fresh seafood, including prawns, mussels and squid rings
1/2 red pepper, deseeded and chopped
1/2 yellow pepper, deseeded and chopped
1 tbsp capers, rinsed
55 g/2 oz Taleggio cheese, grated
3 tbsp freshly grated Parmesan cheese
1/2 tsp dried oregano
75 g/2¾ oz anchovy fillets in oil, drained and sliced
10 black olives, stoned
salt and pepper

Preheat the oven to 220°C/425°F/Gas Mark 7. Prepare the pizza dough according to the packet instructions. Turn out onto a lightly floured work surface and knead for 5 minutes until smooth. Roll out the dough into a 20-cm/8-inch round. Transfer to a lightly oiled baking sheet and push up the edge with your fingers to form a small rim. Leave to stand in a warm place for 10 minutes.

Spread the tomato sauce over the pizza base, almost to the edge. Arrange the mixed seafood, peppers and capers evenly on top.

Sprinkle the cheeses and oregano evenly over the topping. Add the anchovy fillets and olives, drizzle with oil and season to taste with salt and pepper.

Bake in the preheated oven for 20–25 minutes until the crust is crisp and the cheese has melted. Serve immediately.

serves 4 | *prep* 15 minutes | *cook* 25 minutes

SPAGHETTI WITH CLAMS

1 kg/2 lb 4 oz live clams
175 ml/6 fl oz water
175 ml/6 fl oz dry white wine
350 g/12 oz dried spaghetti
5 tbsp olive oil
2 garlic cloves, finely chopped
4 tbsp chopped fresh flat-leaf parsley
salt and pepper

Scrub the clams under cold running water. Discard any with broken shells or any that refuse to close when tapped. Put the clams, water and wine in a large, heavy-based saucepan and cook, covered, over a high heat, shaking the saucepan occasionally, for 3–4 minutes, or until the clams have opened. Discard any clams that remain closed.

Remove the clams with a slotted spoon and set aside to cool slightly. Strain the cooking liquid through a muslin-lined sieve into a small saucepan. Bring to the boil and cook until reduced by about half, then remove from the heat. Meanwhile, remove the clams from their shells and set aside.

Bring a large saucepan of lightly salted water to the boil. Add the pasta, return to the boil and cook for 8–10 minutes until tender but still firm to the bite.

Meanwhile, heat the oil in a large, heavy-based frying pan, add the garlic and cook, stirring frequently, for 2 minutes. Add the parsley and the reduced cooking liquid and simmer gently.

Drain the pasta and add to the frying pan with the clams. Season to taste with salt and pepper and cook, stirring constantly, for 4 minutes until the pasta is coated and the clams have heated through. Transfer to a warmed serving dish and serve immediately.

serves 4 | prep 30 minutes | cook 35 minutes

SEAFOOD RISOTTO

225 g/8 oz raw prawns, in their shells
225 g/8 oz live clams
225 g/8 oz live mussels
2 garlic cloves, halved
1 lemon, sliced
600 ml/1 pint water
115 g/4 oz unsalted butter

1 tbsp olive oil
1 onion, finely chopped
2 tbsp chopped fresh flat-leaf parsley
350 g/12 oz arborio rice
125 ml/4 fl oz dry white wine
225 g /8 oz prepared squid, cut into
   small pieces or rings

4 tbsp Marsala
salt and pepper

Pull the heads off the prawns, then peel off the shells. Wrap the heads and shells in a square of muslin and gently pound with a pestle or the side of a rolling pin, reserving any liquid they may yield. Using a sharp knife, make a slit along the underside of each prawn, then pull out the dark vein and discard. Set the prawns aside until required. Scrub the clams under cold running water. Clean the mussels by scrubbing or scraping the shells and pulling out any beards that are attached to them. Discard any mussels or clams with broken shells or any that refuse to close when tapped. Put into a colander and rinse well under cold running water.

Put the garlic, lemon, mussels and clams in a large, heavy-based saucepan and add the muslin-wrapped shells and any reserved liquid. Pour in the water, cover tightly and bring to the boil over a high heat. Cook, shaking the saucepan occasionally, for 3–4 minutes, or until the mussels and clams have opened. Discard any that remain closed. Transfer the mussels and clams to a bowl and strain the cooking liquid through a muslin-lined sieve into a measuring jug. Make up to 1.2 litres/2 pints with water.

Pour the liquid into a clean saucepan. Bring to the boil, then reduce the heat and simmer gently.

Melt 25 g/1 oz of the butter with the oil in a large, heavy-based saucepan over a low heat, add the onion and half the parsley and cook, stirring occasionally, for 5 minutes until softened. Add the rice and cook, stirring constantly, for 2–3 minutes until all the grains are coated and glistening.

Add the wine and cook, stirring constantly, until it has almost completely evaporated. Add a ladleful of the hot shellfish cooking liquid and cook, still stirring constantly, until it has been absorbed. Continue cooking, stirring and adding the liquid, a ladleful at a time, for 20 minutes, or until the rice is tender and all the liquid has been absorbed.

About 5 minutes before the rice is ready, melt 55 g/2 oz of the remaining butter in a heavy-based saucepan over a medium heat. Add the squid and cook, stirring frequently, for 3 minutes, then add the reserved prawns and cook for a further 2–3 minutes until the squid is opaque and the prawns turn pink. Stir in the Marsala, bring to the boil and cook until all the liquid has evaporated.

Stir the seafood into the rice, add the remaining butter and parsley and season to taste with salt and pepper. Heat through briefly and serve immediately.

serves 6 | *prep 25 minutes, plus 40 minutes' chilling and resting* | *cook 50–55 minutes*

CRAB & WATERCRESS TART

PASTRY
125 g/4½ oz plain flour, plus extra
    for dusting
pinch of salt
75 g/2½ oz cold butter, diced, plus
    extra for greasing
ice-cold water

FILLING
300 g/10½ oz fresh white and brown
    crabmeat, thawed if frozen
1 bunch of watercress, leaves picked
    from the stems
50 ml/2 fl oz milk
2 large eggs plus 3 egg yolks
200 ml/7 fl oz double cream
½ tsp ground nutmeg
½ bunch of fresh chives, snipped
2 tbsp freshly grated Parmesan
    cheese
salt and pepper

Lightly grease a 23-cm/9-inch loose-based fluted tart tin. Sift the flour with the salt into a food processor, add the butter and process until the mixture resembles fine breadcrumbs. Tip the mixture into a large bowl and add a little cold water, just enough to bring the dough together. Turn out onto a lightly floured work surface. Roll out to 8 cm/3¼ inches larger than the tin. Line the tin with the pastry and trim the edge. Line the tart case with baking paper and fill with baking beans. Chill in the refrigerator for 30 minutes. Meanwhile, preheat the oven to 190°C/375°F/Gas Mark 5.

Remove the tart case from the refrigerator and bake in the preheated oven for 10 minutes. Remove the paper and beans and bake the tart case for a further 5 minutes. Remove from the oven and reduce the oven temperature to 160°C/325°F/Gas Mark 3.

Arrange the crabmeat and watercress in the tart case, reserving a few watercress leaves for garnishing. Whisk the milk, eggs and egg yolks together in a bowl. Bring the cream to simmering point in a saucepan and pour over the egg mixture, whisking all the time. Season to taste with salt and pepper and stir in the nutmeg and chives. Carefully pour over the crab and watercress and scatter over the cheese. Bake for 35–40 minutes until golden and set. Leave the tart to rest for 10 minutes before serving, garnished with the reserved watercress.

serves 4–6 | *prep* 20 minutes | *cook* 40 minutes

CRAB SOUFFLE

25 g/1 oz dried breadcrumbs
40 g/1½ oz butter, plus extra
  for greasing
1 small onion, finely chopped
1 garlic clove, crushed
2 tsp mustard powder
25 g/1 oz plain flour
225 ml/8 fl oz milk
50 g/1¾ oz Gruyère cheese, grated
3 eggs, separated
225 g/8 oz fresh crabmeat, thawed
  if frozen
2 tbsp snipped fresh chives
pinch of cayenne pepper
salt and pepper

Preheat the oven to 200°C/400°F/Gas Mark 6. Generously grease a 1.4-litre/2½-pint soufflé dish. Add the breadcrumbs and shake around the dish to coat completely, shaking out any excess. Set aside on a baking tray.

Melt the butter in a large saucepan over a low heat, add the onion and cook, stirring occasionally, for 8 minutes, until softened but not browned. Add the garlic and cook, stirring, for 1 minute. Then add the mustard powder and flour and continue stirring for another minute. Gradually add the milk, stirring constantly, until smooth. Increase the heat slightly and bring slowly to the boil, stirring constantly. Simmer gently for 2 minutes. Remove from the heat and stir in the cheese. Leave to cool slightly.

Lightly beat in the egg yolks, then fold in the crabmeat, chives, cayenne and salt and pepper to taste.

Whisk the egg whites in a clean, grease-free bowl until they hold stiff peaks. Add a large spoonful of the egg whites to the crab mixture and fold together to slacken. Add the remaining egg whites and fold together carefully but thoroughly. Spoon into the prepared dish.

Cook in the preheated oven for 25 minutes until well risen and golden. Serve immediately.

6

Healthful, colourful, flavourful – you simply cannot go wrong with this range of easy yet imaginative fish-based salads. Some are light, refreshing summertime dishes, as you would expect, but others featuring rice, couscous, pasta, noodles and potatoes offer more substantial fare to serve as a main meal at any time of year.

SALADS

Salade Niçoise is a familiar favourite, but there are other variations on the same theme using fresh tuna steaks cooked in moments in a griddle pan. Besides beans, canned and fresh, creamy avocado and tender asparagus spears provide perfect support for the star ingredient. But for a taste of the exotic, try Chinese Prawn Salad, with mango, and Cantaloupe & Crab Salad.

serves 4 | *prep* 25 minutes, plus 6 hours' chilling | *cook* 10 minutes

MACKEREL & POTATO SALAD

125 g/4¹/₂ oz new potatoes, scrubbed
    and diced
225 g/8 oz mackerel fillets, skinned
1.2 litres/2 pints water
1 bay leaf
1 slice of lemon
1 eating apple, cored and diced
1 shallot, thinly sliced
3 tbsp white wine vinegar
1 tsp sunflower oil
1¹/₂ tsp caster sugar
¹/₄ tsp Dijon mustard
salt and pepper

TO SERVE
2 tbsp low-fat natural yogurt
¹/₄ cucumber, thinly sliced
1 bunch of watercress
1 tbsp snipped fresh chives

Steam the potatoes over a saucepan of simmering water for 10 minutes, or until tender. Meanwhile, using a sharp knife, remove the skin from the mackerel fillets and discard. Cut the fish into bite-sized pieces. Bring the water to the boil in a large, shallow saucepan, then reduce the heat so that it is just simmering and add the fish pieces, bay leaf and lemon. Poach for 3 minutes, or until the flesh of the fish is opaque. Remove with a slotted spoon and transfer to a serving dish.

Drain the potatoes and transfer to a large bowl. Add the apple and shallot and mix well, then spoon the mixture over the fish.

Mix the vinegar, oil, sugar and mustard together in a jug, season to taste with salt and pepper and whisk thoroughly. Pour the dressing over the potato mixture. Cover and chill in the refrigerator for up to 6 hours.

To serve, spread the yogurt over the salad, then arrange the cucumber decoratively on top. Add sprigs of watercress and sprinkle with the chives.

serves 4 | *prep* 10 minutes | *cook* 10 minutes

SMOKED HADDOCK SALAD

350 g/12 oz smoked haddock fillet,
  skinned
4 tbsp olive oil
1 tbsp lemon juice
2 tbsp soured cream
1 tbsp hot water
2 tbsp snipped fresh chives, plus extra
  to garnish
1 plum tomato, peeled, deseeded
  and diced
8 quail's eggs
4 thick slices Granary or multigrain
  bread
115 g/4 oz mixed salad leaves
salt and pepper

Fill a large frying pan with water and bring to the boil. Add the smoked haddock fillet, cover and remove the pan from the heat. Leave to stand for 10 minutes until the fish is tender. Remove with a slotted spoon and drain on a plate. Flake the fish, removing and discarding any small bones. Set aside. Discard the cooking liquid.

Meanwhile, whisk the oil, lemon juice, soured cream, hot water, chives and salt and pepper to taste together in a jug. Stir in the tomato. Set aside.

Bring a small saucepan of water to the boil. Carefully lower the quail's eggs into the water and cook for 3–4 minutes from when the water returns to the boil (3 minutes for a slightly soft centre, 4 minutes for a firm centre). Drain immediately and refresh under cold running water. Carefully shell the eggs, cut in half lengthways and set aside.

Toast the bread and put a slice on each of 4 serving plates. Top with the salad leaves, then the flaked fish and finally the quail's eggs. Spoon over the dressing and garnish with a few extra chives.

serves 4 | *prep* 20 minutes, plus 20 minutes' cooling | *cook* 10–12 minutes

SALADE NICOISE

Bring 2 saucepans of water to the boil. Add the eggs to 1 saucepan and return to the boil. Reduce the heat and cook for 10 minutes. Meanwhile, put the beans in the other saucepan. Bring to the boil and blanch for 3 minutes, then drain and plunge into cold water. Drain again and leave to cool. When the eggs are cooked, drain and plunge into cold water. Drain again and leave to cool.

To make the dressing, combine the olive oil, vinegar, honey and garlic in a small bowl. Season to taste with salt and pepper and stir well together.

Divide the pepper, tomatoes, onion, parsley and coriander between 4 serving dishes. Halve the olives and the beans, shell and quarter the eggs and add them all to the salad. Drain the tuna and anchovies and add to the salad. Drizzle over the dressing and garnish with capers and parsley sprigs. Cover with clingfilm and chill in the refrigerator until required.

4 eggs
200 g/7 oz French beans
1 green pepper, deseeded and sliced
4 tomatoes, cut into wedges
1 red onion, halved and sliced
1 tbsp chopped fresh parsley
1 tbsp chopped fresh coriander
50 g/1¾ oz black olives, stoned
400 g/14 oz canned tuna in brine
50 g/1¾ oz anchovy fillets in oil

DRESSING
5 tbsp extra virgin olive oil
3 tbsp red wine vinegar
½ tsp honey
1 garlic clove, chopped
salt and pepper

TO GARNISH
capers, rinsed
fresh parsley sprigs

serves 4 | *prep* 15 minutes | *cook* 30 minutes

MOROCCAN COUSCOUS SALAD

225 g/8 oz couscous
1 cinnamon stick, about 5 cm/
  2 inches long
2 tsp coriander seeds
1 tsp cumin seeds
2 tbsp olive oil
1 small onion, finely chopped
2 garlic cloves, finely chopped
1/2 tsp ground turmeric
pinch of cayenne pepper
1 tbsp lemon juice
50 g/1 3/4 oz sultanas
3 ripe plum tomatoes, chopped
85 g/3 oz cucumber, chopped
4 spring onions, sliced
200 g/7 oz canned tuna in olive oil,
  drained and flaked
3 tbsp chopped fresh coriander
salt and pepper

Prepare the couscous according to the packet instructions, omitting any butter. Transfer to a large bowl and set aside.

Heat a small, dry frying pan over a high heat and add the cinnamon stick, coriander seeds and cumin seeds. Cook, shaking the pan frequently, until the seeds begin to pop and smell fragrant. Remove from the heat and pour the seeds into a mortar. Grind with a pestle to a fine powder. Alternatively, grind in a spice grinder. Set aside.

Heat the oil in a clean frying pan over a low heat, add the onion and cook, stirring frequently, for 7–8 minutes until softened and lightly browned. Add the garlic and cook, stirring, for a further minute. Stir in the roasted and ground spices, turmeric and cayenne pepper and cook, stirring, for a further minute. Remove from the heat and stir in the lemon juice. Add this mixture to the couscous and mix together well, ensuring that all of the grains are coated.

Add the sultanas, tomatoes, cucumber, spring onions, tuna and coriander. Season to taste with salt and pepper and mix together. Leave to cool completely. Serve at room temperature.

serves 4 | *prep* 10 minutes | *cook* 5–10 minutes

WARM TUNA & KIDNEY BEAN SALAD

4 fresh tuna steaks, about 175 g/
  6 oz each
1 tbsp olive oil
200 g/7 oz canned kidney beans
100 g/3¹/₂ oz canned sweetcorn
  kernels
2 spring onions, thinly sliced
salt and pepper

DRESSING
5 tbsp extra virgin olive oil
3 tbsp balsamic vinegar
1 tbsp lime juice
1 garlic clove, chopped
1 tbsp chopped fresh coriander
salt and pepper

TO GARNISH
fresh coriander sprigs
lime wedges

Heat a ridged griddle pan over a high heat. Lightly brush the tuna steaks with olive oil, then season to taste with salt and pepper. Cook the steaks for 2 minutes, then turn over and cook on the other side for a further 2 minutes for rare or up to 4 minutes for well done. Remove from the heat and leave to cool slightly.

Meanwhile, heat the beans and sweetcorn according to the can instructions, then drain.

To make the dressing, put all the dressing ingredients in a small bowl. Stir together well.

Put the beans, sweetcorn and spring onions in a large bowl, pour over half the dressing and mix together well. Divide the bean and sweetcorn salad between 4 individual serving plates, then top each one with a tuna steak. Drizzle over the remaining dressing, garnish with coriander sprigs and lime wedges and serve immediately.

serves 4–6 | *prep* 15 minutes | *cook* 12 minutes

TUNA & TWO-BEAN SALAD

200 g/7 oz French beans
400 g/14 oz canned small white
   beans, such as cannellini, rinsed
   and drained
4 spring onions, finely chopped
2 fresh tuna steaks, about 225 g/8 oz
   each and 2 cm/³/₄ inch thick
olive oil, for brushing
250 g/9 oz cherry tomatoes, halved
lettuce leaves
fresh mint and parsley sprigs,
   to garnish
country-style crusty bread, to serve

DRESSING
handful of fresh mint leaves, shredded
handful of fresh parsley leaves,
   chopped
1 garlic clove, crushed
4 tbsp extra virgin olive oil
1 tbsp red wine vinegar
salt and pepper

First, make the dressing. Put the mint leaves, parsley leaves, garlic, olive oil and vinegar into a screw-top jar, add salt and pepper to taste and shake until blended. Pour into a large bowl and set aside.

Bring a saucepan of lightly salted water to the boil. Add the French beans and cook for 3 minutes. Add the white beans and cook for a further 4 minutes until the French beans are tender-crisp and the white beans are heated through. Drain well and add to the bowl with the dressing and spring onions. Toss together.

To cook the tuna, heat a ridged griddle pan over a high heat. Lightly brush the tuna steaks with oil, then season to taste with salt and pepper. Cook the steaks for 2 minutes, then turn over and cook on the other side for a further 2 minutes for rare or up to 4 minutes for well done.

Remove the tuna from the griddle pan and leave to rest for 2 minutes, or until completely cool. When ready to serve, add the tomatoes to the bean mixture and toss lightly. Line a serving platter with lettuce leaves and pile on the bean salad. Flake the tuna over the top. Serve warm or at room temperature with plenty of bread, garnished with the herbs.

serves 4 | *prep* 15 minutes | *cook* 15 minutes

TUNA & HERBED FUSILLI SALAD

200 g/7 oz dried fusilli
1 red pepper, deseeded
   and quartered
150 g/5½ oz asparagus spears
1 red onion, sliced
4 tomatoes, sliced
200 g/7 oz canned tuna in brine,
   drained and flaked

DRESSING
6 tbsp basil-flavoured oil or
   extra virgin olive oil
3 tbsp white wine vinegar
1 tbsp lime juice
1 tsp mustard
1 tsp honey
4 tbsp chopped fresh basil, plus extra
   sprigs to garnish

Bring a large saucepan of lightly salted water to the boil. Add the pasta, return to the boil and cook for 8–10 minutes until tender but still firm to the bite.

Meanwhile, put the pepper quarters under a preheated hot grill and cook for 10–12 minutes until the skins begin to blacken. Transfer to a polythene bag, seal and set aside.

Bring a separate saucepan of water to the boil, add the asparagus and blanch for 4 minutes. Drain and plunge into cold water, then drain again. Remove the pasta from the heat, drain and set aside to cool. Remove the pepper quarters from the bag and peel off the skins. Slice the pepper into strips.

To make the dressing, put all the dressing ingredients in a large bowl and stir together well. Add the pasta, pepper strips, asparagus, onion, tomatoes and tuna. Toss together gently, then divide between serving bowls. Garnish with basil sprigs and serve.

serves 4 | *prep* 20 minutes | *cook* no cooking required

SMOKED SALMON & WILD ROCKET SALAD

50 g/1¾ oz wild rocket leaves
1 tbsp chopped fresh flat-leaf parsley
2 spring onions, finely diced
2 large avocados
1 tbsp lemon juice
250 g/9 oz smoked salmon
lime wedges, to serve

LIME MAYONNAISE
150 ml/5 fl oz mayonnaise
2 tbsp lime juice
finely grated rind of 1 lime
1 tbsp chopped fresh flat-leaf parsley,
   plus extra sprigs to garnish

Shred the rocket and arrange in 4 individual salad bowls or on 4 small plates. Scatter over the chopped parsley and spring onions.

Halve, peel and stone the avocados and cut into thin slices or small chunks. Brush with the lemon juice to prevent discolouration, then divide between the salad bowls. Mix together gently. Cut the smoked salmon into strips and scatter over the top.

Put the mayonnaise in a bowl, then add the lime juice and rind and the chopped parsley. Mix together well. Spoon some of the lime mayonnaise on top of each salad, garnish with parsley sprigs and serve with lime wedges for squeezing over.

serves 4 | *prep* 15 minutes | *cook* 5 minutes

SMOKED SALMON, ASPARAGUS & AVOCADO SALAD

200 g/7 oz asparagus spears
1 large avocado
1 tbsp lemon juice
large handful of rocket leaves
225 g/8 oz smoked salmon
1 red onion, finely sliced
1 tbsp chopped fresh flat-leaf parsley,
    plus extra sprigs to garnish
1 tbsp snipped fresh chives
lemon wedges, to garnish
wholemeal bread, to serve

DRESSING
1 garlic clove, chopped
4 tbsp extra virgin olive oil
2 tbsp white wine vinegar
1 tbsp lemon juice
pinch of sugar
1 tsp mustard

Bring a large saucepan of salted water to the boil, add the asparagus and blanch for 4 minutes. Drain and plunge into cold water, then drain again. Set aside to cool.

To make the dressing, combine all the dressing ingredients in a small bowl and stir together well. Halve, peel and stone the avocado and cut into bite-sized pieces. Brush with the lemon juice to prevent discolouration.

To assemble the salad, arrange the rocket leaves on individual serving plates and top with the asparagus and avocado. Cut the smoked salmon into strips and arrange over the top of the salads, then scatter over the onion and herbs. Drizzle over the dressing, then garnish with parsley sprigs and lemon wedges. Serve with wholemeal bread.

serves 4 | *prep* 10 minutes, plus 10 minutes' cooling | *cook* 35 minutes

PRAWN & RICE SALAD

175 g/6 oz mixed long-grain and
   wild rice
350 g/12 oz cooked peeled prawns
1 mango, peeled, stoned and diced
4 spring onions, sliced
25 g/1 oz flaked almonds
1 tbsp finely chopped fresh mint
salt and pepper

DRESSING
1 tbsp extra virgin olive oil
2 tsp lime juice
1 garlic clove, crushed
1 tsp runny honey
salt and pepper

Bring a large saucepan of lightly salted water to the boil. Add the rice, return to the boil and cook for 35 minutes, or until tender. Drain, then transfer to a large bowl and stir in the prawns.

To make the dressing, combine the olive oil, lime juice, garlic and honey in a large jug, season to taste with salt and pepper, and whisk until well blended. Pour the dressing over the rice and prawn mixture and leave to cool.

Add the mango, spring onions, almonds and mint to the salad and season to taste with pepper. Stir thoroughly, transfer to a large serving dish and serve.

serves 4 | *prep* 10 minutes | *cook* 15 minutes

CHINESE PRAWN SALAD

250 g/9 oz dried fine egg noodles
3 tbsp sunflower oil
1 tbsp sesame oil
1 tbsp sesame seeds
150 g/5½ oz beansprouts
1 mango, peeled, stoned and sliced
6 spring onions, sliced
75 g/2¾ oz radishes, sliced
350 g/12 oz cooked peeled prawns
2 tbsp light soy sauce
1 tbsp sherry

Put the noodles in a large, heatproof bowl and pour over enough boiling water to cover. Leave to stand for 10 minutes.

Drain the noodles thoroughly and pat dry with kitchen paper.

Heat the sunflower oil in a large, preheated wok. Add the noodles and stir-fry for 5 minutes, tossing frequently.

Remove the wok from the heat and add the sesame oil, sesame seeds and beansprouts, tossing to mix well.

Mix the mango, spring onions, radishes, prawns, soy sauce and sherry together in a separate bowl.

Toss the prawn mixture with the noodles. Alternatively, arrange the noodles around the edge of a serving plate and pile the prawn mixture into the centre. Serve immediately.

serves 4 | prep 15 minutes | cook 5 minutes

THAI NOODLE SALAD WITH PRAWNS

Put the noodles in a large, heatproof bowl and pour over enough boiling water to cover. Leave to stand for about 4 minutes, or until soft. Drain and rinse under cold running water. Drain again and set aside.

Bring a saucepan of water to the boil. Add the mangetout, return to the boil and blanch for 1 minute. Drain and rinse under cold running water until cold. Drain again and set aside.

Whisk the lime juice, fish sauce, sugar, ginger, chilli and coriander together in a large bowl. Stir in the cucumber and spring onions. Add the drained noodles, mangetout and peeled prawns. Toss the salad gently together.

Divide the noodle salad between 4 large plates. Sprinkle with chopped coriander and the peanuts, if using, then garnish each plate with a whole prawn and a slice of lemon. Serve immediately.

85 g/3 oz dried rice vermicelli noodles
  or rice sticks
175 g/6 oz mangetout, cut crossways
  in half if large
5 tbsp lime juice
4 tbsp Thai fish sauce
1 tbsp sugar, or to taste
2.5-cm/1-inch piece fresh root ginger,
  finely chopped
1 fresh red chilli, deseeded and thinly
  sliced diagonally
4 tbsp chopped fresh coriander or
  mint, plus extra to garnish
10-cm/4-inch piece cucumber, peeled,
  deseeded and diced
2 spring onions, thinly sliced
  diagonally
16–20 large cooked peeled prawns
2 tbsp chopped unsalted peanuts or
  cashew nuts (optional)

TO GARNISH
4 cooked prawns, in their shells
lemon slices

serves 4 | *prep* 15 minutes, plus 45 minutes' chilling | *cook* 6–8 minutes

SEAFOOD SALAD

250 g/9 oz live mussels
350 g/12 oz live scallops, shucked
   and cleaned
250 g/9 oz prepared squid, cut into
   rings and tentacles
1 red onion, halved and finely sliced
300 g/10½ oz asparagus spears,
   blanched and cut into small pieces

DRESSING
4 tbsp extra virgin olive oil
2 tbsp white wine vinegar
1 tbsp lemon juice
1 garlic clove, finely chopped
1 tbsp chopped fresh flat-leaf parsley,
   plus extra sprigs to garnish
salt and pepper

TO GARNISH
lemon wedges
capers, rinsed (optional)
whole cooked baby squid (optional)

Clean the mussels by scrubbing or scraping the shells and pulling out any beards that are attached to them. Discard any with broken shells or any that refuse to close when tapped. Put the mussels in a colander and rinse well under cold running water. Put them in a large saucepan with just the water that clings to their shells and cook, covered, over a high heat, shaking the saucepan occasionally, for 3–4 minutes, or until the mussels have opened. Discard any mussels that remain closed. Strain the mussels, reserving the cooking liquid. Refresh the mussels under cold running water, drain and set aside.

Return the reserved cooking liquid to the saucepan and bring to the boil, add the scallops and squid and cook for 3 minutes. Remove from the heat and drain. Refresh under cold running water and drain again. Remove the mussels from their shells. Put them in a bowl with the scallops and squid and leave to cool. Cover with clingfilm and chill in the refrigerator for 45 minutes.

Divide the seafood between 4 serving plates. Top with the onion and asparagus. Combine all the dressing ingredients in a small bowl, then drizzle over the salad. Garnish with parsley sprigs and lemon wedges, and capers and whole baby squid, if desired.

serves 4 | prep 25 minutes, plus 45 minutes' chilling | cook 10 minutes

SEAFOOD & SPINACH SALAD

Put the mussels in a large saucepan with a little water and cook, covered, over a high heat, shaking the saucepan occasionally, for 3–4 minutes, or until the mussels have opened. Discard any mussels that remain closed. Strain the mussels, reserving the cooking liquid.

Return the reserved cooking liquid to the saucepan and bring to the boil, add the prawns and scallops and cook for 3 minutes. Remove from the heat and drain. Remove the mussels from their shells. Refresh the mussels, prawns and scallops under cold running water, drain and put them in a large bowl. Leave to cool, then cover with clingfilm and chill in the refrigerator for 45 minutes.

Meanwhile, rinse the spinach leaves and transfer them to a saucepan with the water. Cook over a high heat for 1 minute. Transfer to a colander, refresh under cold running water and drain.

To make the dressing, combine all the dressing ingredients in a small bowl. Divide the spinach between 4 serving dishes, then scatter over half the spring onions. Top with the mussels, prawns and scallops, then scatter over the remaining spring onions. Drizzle over the dressing, garnish with coriander sprigs and lemon wedges and serve.

500 g/1 lb 2 oz live mussels, scrubbed
   and debearded
100 g/3½ oz raw prawns, peeled
   and deveined
350 g/12 oz live scallops, shucked
   and cleaned
500 g/1 lb 2 oz baby spinach leaves
4 tbsp water
3 spring onions, sliced
lemon wedges, to garnish

DRESSING
4 tbsp extra virgin olive oil
2 tbsp white wine vinegar
1 tbsp lemon juice
1 tsp finely grated lemon rind
1 garlic clove, chopped
1 tbsp grated fresh root ginger
1 small fresh red chilli, deseeded
   and sliced
1 tbsp chopped fresh coriander, plus
   extra sprigs to garnish
salt and pepper

serves 4 | *prep* 10 minutes, plus 30 minutes' chilling | *cook* no cooking required

CRAB & CITRUS SALSA

250 g/9 oz canned or fresh crabmeat, drained if canned and thawed if frozen, flaked
1 red pepper, deseeded and chopped
4 tomatoes, chopped
3 spring onions, chopped
1 tbsp chopped fresh flat-leaf parsley, plus extra sprigs to garnish
1 fresh red chilli, deseeded and chopped
3 tbsp lime juice
3 tbsp orange juice
salt and pepper
lime wedges, to garnish

TO SERVE
carrot batons
celery batons
tortilla chips

Put the crabmeat, pepper, tomatoes, spring onions, parsley and chilli in a large, non-metallic bowl. Add the lime juice and orange juice, season to taste with salt and pepper and mix well. Cover with clingfilm and chill in the refrigerator for 30 minutes to allow the flavours to combine.

Remove the salsa from the refrigerator. Garnish with parsley sprigs and lime wedges and serve with carrot and celery batons and tortilla chips for dipping.

serves 4 | *prep* 15 minutes | *cook* no cooking required

CANTALOUPE & CRAB SALAD

350 g/12 oz fresh crabmeat, thawed
  if frozen
5 tbsp low-fat mayonnaise
50 ml/2 fl oz low-fat natural yogurt
4 tsp extra virgin olive oil
4 tsp lime juice
1 spring onion, finely chopped
4 tsp finely chopped fresh flat-leaf
  parsley, plus extra sprigs to garnish
pinch of cayenne pepper
1 cantaloupe melon
2 radicchio heads, separated
  into leaves

Put the crabmeat in a large bowl and pick over it very carefully to remove any remaining shell or cartilage, but try not to break the meat up.

Put the mayonnaise, yogurt, oil, lime juice, spring onion, chopped parsley and cayenne pepper in a separate bowl and mix together until well blended. Fold in the crabmeat.

Halve the melon and remove and discard the seeds. Thinly slice, then cut off the rind with a sharp knife.

Arrange the melon slices and radicchio leaves on 4 large serving plates, then arrange the crabmeat mixture on top. Garnish with a few parsley sprigs and serve.

7

Fish takes centre stage in this next selection of recipes, providing simple yet sophisticated dishes for entertaining in high style and everyday meals for family and friends. Along with such fish staples as salmon, trout, cod and plaice, skate, hake, sole, monkfish, red snapper and John Dory all make a unique culinary contribution.

HEARTY MAIN DISHES

Fish pie never loses its appeal, and here you can enjoy it in its many guises – cloaked in rich pastry in Salmon Coulibiac and Flaky Pastry Fish Pie, or topped with crisp-baked, creamy mash in Fisherman's Pie. But you may be looking for something more challenging on the taste buds, in which case Thai-style Fish Curry with Rice Noodles, aromatic Moroccan Fish Tagine and piquant Whole Fried Fish with Soy & Ginger are sure to satisfy.

serves 4 | prep 15 minutes | cook 35–50 minutes

BAKED MACKEREL STUFFED
WITH RAISINS & PINE KERNELS

3 tbsp olive oil, plus extra for oiling
1 onion, finely chopped
100 g/3¹/₂ oz fresh breadcrumbs
55 g/2 oz raisins, chopped
100 g/3¹/₂ oz pine kernels
grated rind and juice of 1 lemon
1 tbsp chopped fresh dill
2 tbsp chopped fresh flat-leaf parsley
1 egg, beaten
4 mackerel, cleaned, about 350 g/
   12 oz each
salt and pepper
lemon wedges, to garnish

Preheat the oven to 190°C/375°F/Gas Mark 5. Oil a shallow ovenproof dish large enough to hold the fish in a single layer.

To make the stuffing, heat 2 tablespoons of the oil in a large, heavy-based frying pan, add the onion and cook, stirring frequently, for 5 minutes until softened. Remove from the heat.

Put the breadcrumbs, raisins, pine kernels, lemon rind, dill, parsley and salt and pepper to taste in a large bowl. Add the onion and egg and mix well together.

Press the stuffing mixture into the cavity of the fish and transfer to the prepared dish. Using a sharp knife, make diagonal slashes along each fish. Drizzle over the lemon juice and the remaining oil.

Bake the fish, uncovered, in the preheated oven, basting twice during cooking, for 30–45 minutes until tender. Serve hot, garnished with lemon wedges.

serves 4 | *prep* 30 minutes | *cook* 45–50 minutes

SALMON COULIBIAC

50 g/1¾ oz long-grain white rice
3 eggs
2 tbsp vegetable oil
1 onion, finely chopped
1 garlic clove, crushed
1 tsp finely grated lemon rind
2 tbsp chopped fresh parsley
1 tbsp chopped fresh dill
450 g/1 lb salmon fillet, skinned
  and cubed
500 g/1 lb 2 oz ready-made
  puff pastry

plain flour, for dusting
beaten egg, for sealing
  and glazing

QUICK HOLLANDAISE SAUCE
175 g/6 oz butter, plus extra
  for greasing
1 tbsp wine vinegar
2 tbsp lemon juice
3 egg yolks
salt and pepper

Preheat the oven to 200°C/400°F/Gas Mark 6. Lightly grease a baking tray. Bring a saucepan of lightly salted water to the boil. Add the rice, return to the boil and cook for 7–8 minutes until tender. Drain well and set aside. Meanwhile, bring a small saucepan of water to the boil. Add the eggs, return to the boil and cook for 8 minutes. Drain and refresh under cold water. When cool enough to handle, shell and slice thinly.

Heat the oil in a frying pan over a medium heat, add the onion and cook, stirring frequently, for 5 minutes until softened. Add the garlic and cook, stirring, for a further 30 seconds. Add to the rice with the lemon rind, parsley, dill and salmon.

Roll out the pastry on a lightly floured work surface to a rectangle measuring 40 x 30 cm/16 x 12 inches. Transfer to the prepared baking tray. Spoon half the filling onto one half of the pastry, leaving a border about 2 cm/¾ inch. Top with the sliced eggs, then the remaining filling.

Dampen the outside edges of the pastry with a little beaten egg, then fold over the remaining pastry. Crimp the edges to seal well. Mark the pastry using a small sharp knife, taking care not to cut through the pastry. Decorate with pastry trimmings and brush with beaten egg.

Bake in the preheated oven for 30–35 minutes until risen and golden.

To make the sauce, melt the butter in a small saucepan over a low heat. Put the vinegar and lemon juice in a separate saucepan and bring to the boil. Meanwhile, put the egg yolks and a pinch of salt in a blender or food processor and combine. With the motor running, gradually add the hot vinegar and lemon juice through the feed tube. When the butter starts to bubble, pour it in a steady stream into the machine until it has all been added and the sauce has thickened. Season to taste with salt and pepper. Transfer to a heatproof bowl set over a saucepan of hot water to keep warm.

Serve the pie hot with the sauce.

serves 4 | *prep* 15 minutes | *cook* 5–6 minutes

SALMON STEAKS WITH GREEN SAUCE

4 salmon fillets, about 140 g/5 oz
  each, skinned
2 tbsp olive oil
salt and pepper

GREEN SAUCE
70 g/2¹/₂ oz fresh flat-leaf
  parsley sprigs
8 large fresh basil leaves
2 fresh oregano sprigs or ¹/₂ tsp dried
3–4 canned anchovy fillets in oil,
  drained and chopped
2 tsp capers, rinsed
1 shallot, chopped
1 large garlic clove
2–3 tsp lemon juice, to taste
125 ml/4 fl oz extra virgin olive oil

To make the sauce, put the parsley, basil, oregano, anchovies, capers, shallot, garlic and lemon juice in a food processor and process until chopped. With the motor running, slowly add the extra virgin olive oil through the feed tube. Taste and adjust the seasoning, if necessary, remembering that the anchovies and capers are salty in themselves. Pour into a serving bowl, cover with clingfilm and chill in the refrigerator until required.

When ready to serve, brush the salmon fillets on both sides with the olive oil and season to taste with salt and pepper. Heat a large frying pan over a high heat until you can feel the heat rising from the surface. Cook the salmon steaks for 3 minutes, then turn over and cook on the other side for 2–3 minutes until they feel springy and the flesh flakes easily.

Serve the hot salmon steaks with a little of the chilled sauce spooned over.

serves 6 | *prep* 15 minutes, plus 15 minutes–2 hours' cooling | *cook* 50 minutes–1 hour

POACHED SALMON

melted butter, for brushing
1 whole fresh salmon, about 1.8 kg/
  4 lb, cleaned and scaled
1 lemon, sliced
few fresh parsley sprigs, plus extra
  to garnish
125 ml/4 fl oz white wine or water
salt and pepper
lemon wedges, to garnish

HOLLANDAISE SAUCE
2 tbsp white wine vinegar
2 tbsp water
6 black peppercorns
3 egg yolks
250 g/9 oz unsalted butter
2 tsp lemon juice
salt and pepper

Preheat the oven to 150°C/300°F/Gas Mark 2. Line a large roasting tin with a double layer of foil and brush with butter.

Trim off the fins, then season the salmon to taste with salt and pepper, inside and out. Lay on the foil and put the lemon slices and parsley in the body cavity. Pour over the wine and gather up the foil to make a fairly loose parcel.

Bake in the preheated oven for 50–60 minutes. Test the salmon with the point of a knife – the flesh should flake when the fish is cooked. Remove from the oven and leave to stand for 15 minutes before removing from the foil to serve hot. To serve cold, leave for 1–2 hours until lukewarm, then carefully remove from the foil and peel away the skin from the top side, leaving the head and tail intact.

Meanwhile, to make the sauce, put the vinegar, water and peppercorns in a small saucepan and bring to the boil, then reduce the heat and simmer until it is reduced to 1 tablespoon (take care – this happens very quickly). Sieve the vinegar and discard the peppercorns.

Put the egg yolks in a blender or food processor and process to blend. With the motor running, add the vinegar through the feed tube. Melt the butter in a small saucepan over a high heat and heat until it almost turns brown. Again, while the motor is running, add three-quarters of the butter, the lemon juice, then the remaining butter through the feed tube. Season well with salt and pepper.

Transfer the sauce to a serving bowl or keep warm for up to 1 hour in a heatproof bowl set over a saucepan of hot water. To serve cold, leave to cool, cover and store in the refrigerator for up to 2 days. Serve the sauce on the side with the salmon, garnished with parsley sprigs and lemon wedges.

serves 4 | *prep* 10 minutes, plus 15 minutes' soaking | *cook* 15–20 minutes

COD WITH CATALAN SPINACH

4 cod fillets, about 175 g/6 oz each
olive oil
salt and pepper
lemon wedges, to serve

CATALAN SPINACH
55 g/2 oz raisins
55 g/2 oz pine kernels
4 tbsp extra virgin olive oil
3 garlic cloves, crushed
500 g/1 lb 2 oz baby spinach leaves,
  rinsed and shaken dry

To make the Catalan Spinach, put the raisins in a small bowl, cover with hot water and set aside to soak for 15 minutes. Drain well.

Meanwhile, put the pine kernels in a frying pan over a medium-high heat and dry-fry, shaking the pan frequently, for 1–2 minutes until toasted and golden brown – watch closely because they burn quickly.

Heat the extra virgin olive oil in a large frying pan with a tight-fitting lid over a medium–high heat, add the garlic and cook, stirring, for 2 minutes, or until golden but not browned. Remove with a slotted spoon and discard.

Add the spinach to the oil with only the water that clings to the leaves. Cover and cook for 4–5 minutes until wilted. Uncover, stir in the raisins and pine kernels and continue cooking until all the liquid evaporates. Season to taste with salt and pepper and keep warm.

Brush the cod fillets lightly with olive oil and sprinkle with salt and pepper to taste. Put under a preheated hot grill about 10 cm/4 inches from the heat and grill for 8–10 minutes until the flesh is opaque and flakes easily.

Divide the spinach between 4 serving plates and arrange the cod fillets on top. Serve with lemon wedges for squeezing over.

serves 4–6 | *prep* 25 minutes | *cook* 35–45 minutes

FLAKY PASTRY FISH PIE

650 g/1 lb 7 oz white fish fillets, such
   as cod or haddock, skinned
300 ml/10 fl oz milk
1 bay leaf
4 peppercorns
1 small onion, finely sliced
40 g/1½ oz butter, plus extra
   for greasing
40 g/1½ oz plain flour, plus extra
   for dusting
1 tbsp chopped fresh parsley
   or tarragon
150 ml/5 fl oz single cream
2 hard-boiled eggs, roughly chopped
400 g/14 oz ready-made puff pastry
1 egg, beaten
salt and pepper

Preheat the oven to 200°C/400°F/Gas Mark 6.
Grease a 1.2-litre/2-pint pie dish.

Put the fish in a frying pan and cover with the milk.
Add the bay leaf, peppercorns and onion slices.
Bring to the boil, then reduce the heat and simmer
gently for 10–12 minutes.

Remove from the heat and strain off the milk into a
measuring jug. Add a little extra milk, if necessary,
to make up to 300 ml/10 fl oz. Flake the fish into
large pieces, removing and discarding any bones.

Melt the butter in a saucepan over a low heat,
add the flour and cook, stirring constantly, for
2–3 minutes. Remove from the heat and gradually
stir in the reserved milk, beating well after each
addition. Return the saucepan to the heat and cook,
stirring constantly, until thickened. Cook for a

further 2–3 minutes until smooth and glossy. Add
the herbs, cream and salt and pepper to taste.

Put the fish in the pie dish, then add the hard-boiled
eggs and season to taste with salt and pepper. Pour
the sauce over the fish and mix carefully.

Roll out the pastry on a lightly floured work surface
until just larger than the pie dish. Cut off a strip
1 cm/½ inch wide from around the edge. Moisten
the rim of the dish with water and press the pastry
strip onto it. Moisten the pastry collar and put on
the pastry lid. Crimp the edges to seal well. If
desired, garnish with the pastry trimmings shaped
into leaves. Brush with the beaten egg.

Put the pie on a baking tray and bake near the top
of the preheated oven for 20–25 minutes. Cover
with foil if it begins to get too brown.

serves 4 | *prep* 15 minutes | *cook* 25 minutes

MONKFISH PARCELS

4 tsp olive oil
2 courgettes, sliced
1 large red pepper, peeled, deseeded
   and cut into strips
2 monkfish fillets, about 125 g/4 1/2 oz
   each, skin and membrane removed
6 smoked streaky bacon rashers
salt and pepper

TO SERVE
freshly cooked pasta
slices of olive bread

Preheat the oven to 190°C/375°F/Gas Mark 5.
Cut 4 large pieces of foil, about 23 cm/
9 inches square. Brush lightly with a little of
the oil, then divide the courgettes and
pepper between them.

Rinse the fish fillets under cold running water
and pat dry with kitchen paper. Cut them in
half, then put 1 piece on top of each pile of
courgettes and pepper. Cut the bacon rashers
in half and lay 3 pieces across each piece of
fish. Season to taste with salt and pepper,
drizzle over the remaining oil and close up the
parcels. Seal tightly, transfer to an ovenproof
dish and bake in the preheated oven for
25 minutes.

Remove from the oven, open each foil parcel
slightly and serve with pasta and slices of
olive bread.

serves 4 | *prep* 15 minutes | *cook* 10 minutes

FISH CURRY WITH RICE NOODLES

2 tbsp vegetable or groundnut oil
1 large onion, chopped
2 garlic cloves, chopped
85 g/3 oz button mushrooms
225 g/8 oz monkfish, cut into
  2.5-cm/1-inch cubes
225 g/8 oz salmon fillets, cut into
  2.5-cm/1-inch cubes
225 g/8 oz cod fillets, cut into 2.5-cm/
  1-inch cubes
2 tbsp Thai red curry paste
400 g/14 oz canned coconut milk
handful of fresh coriander, chopped
1 tsp palm sugar or soft light
  brown sugar
1 tsp Thai fish sauce
115 g/4 oz dried rice noodles
3 spring onions, chopped
50 g/2 oz beansprouts
few fresh Thai basil leaves

Heat the oil in a preheated wok or large frying pan over a medium heat, add the onion, garlic and mushrooms and cook, stirring frequently, for 5 minutes until softened but not browned.

Add the fish, curry paste and coconut milk and bring gently to the boil. Simmer for 2–3 minutes before adding half the coriander, and the sugar and fish sauce. Keep warm.

Meanwhile, soak the noodles in enough boiling water to cover in a heatproof bowl for 3–4 minutes until tender, or cook according to the packet instructions. Drain well through a metal colander. Put the colander and noodles over a saucepan of simmering water. Add the spring onions, beansprouts and most of the basil and steam on top of the noodles for 1–2 minutes until just wilted.

Pile the noodles onto warmed serving plates and top with the fish curry. Scatter the remaining coriander and basil over the top and serve immediately.

serves 4 | *prep* 10 minutes | *cook* 50 minutes–1 hour 5 minutes

MOROCCAN FISH TAGINE

2 tbsp olive oil
1 large onion, finely chopped
large pinch of saffron threads
1/2 tsp ground cinnamon
1 tsp ground coriander
1/2 tsp ground cumin
1/2 tsp ground turmeric
200 g/7 oz canned chopped tomatoes
300 ml/10 fl oz fish stock
4 small red mullet, cleaned, boned
   and heads and tails removed
50 g/1 3/4 oz stoned green olives
1 tbsp chopped preserved lemon
3 tbsp chopped fresh coriander
salt and pepper
freshly prepared couscous, to serve

Heat the oil in a large saucepan or flameproof casserole over a low heat, add the onion and cook, stirring occasionally, for 10 minutes until softened but not browned. Add the saffron, cinnamon, coriander, cumin and turmeric and cook, stirring, for a further 30 seconds.

Add the tomatoes and stock and stir well. Bring to the boil, then reduce the heat, cover and simmer for 15 minutes. Uncover and simmer for a further 20–35 minutes until thickened.

Cut each mullet in half, then add the pieces to the saucepan, pushing them into the sauce. Simmer gently for a further 5–6 minutes until the fish is just cooked.

Carefully stir in the olives, preserved lemon and coriander. Season to taste with salt and pepper and serve with couscous.

serves 2 | *prep* 15 minutes | *cook* 50 minutes

FLOUNDER FOR TWO

150 ml/5 fl oz olive oil
375 g/13 oz waxy potatoes, peeled
    and thinly sliced
1 fennel bulb, thinly sliced
2 large tomatoes, grilled, peeled,
    deseeded and chopped
2 shallots, sliced
1–2 whole flounders, cleaned, about
    1.3 kg/3 lb
4 tbsp dry white wine
2 tbsp finely chopped fresh parsley
salt and pepper
lemon wedges, to serve

Preheat the oven to 200°C/400°F/Gas Mark 6. Spread 4 tablespoons of the oil over the base of a shallow roasting tin large enough to hold the flounder. Arrange the potatoes in a single layer, then top with the fennel, tomatoes and shallots. Season to taste with salt and pepper. Drizzle with a further 4 tablespoons of the oil. Roast the vegetables in the preheated oven for 30 minutes.

Season the fish to taste with salt and pepper and put on top of the vegetables. Sprinkle with the wine and the remaining oil.

Return the roasting tin to the oven and roast the fish, uncovered, for 20 minutes, or until the flesh flakes easily.

To serve, skin the fish and remove the fillets. Sprinkle the parsley over the vegetables. Arrange 2–4 fillets on each plate, with the vegetables spooned alongside, accompanied by the lemon wedges for squeezing over.

serves 4 | *prep* 10 minutes | *cook* 15 minutes

JOHN DORY EN PAPILLOTE

2 John Dory, filleted
115 g/4 oz stoned black olives
12 cherry tomatoes, halved
115 g/4 oz French beans
handful of fresh basil leaves, plus
   extra to garnish
4 lemon slices
4 tsp olive oil
salt and pepper
boiled new potatoes, to serve

Preheat the oven to 200°C/400°F/Gas Mark 6. Wash and dry the fish fillets and set aside. Cut 4 large rectangles of baking paper, each measuring about 46 x 30 cm/18 x 12 inches. Fold in half to make a 23 x 30-cm/9 x 12-inch rectangle. Cut this into a large heart shape and open out.

Lay a John Dory fillet on one half of the paper heart. Top with a quarter of the olives, tomatoes, beans, basil and 1 lemon slice. Drizzle over 1 teaspoon of the oil and season well with salt and pepper.

Fold over the other half of the paper and bring the edges of the paper together to enclose. Repeat to make 4 parcels.

Put the parcels on a baking tray and cook in the preheated oven for 15 minutes, or until the fish is tender.

Transfer each parcel to a serving plate, unopened, allowing your guests to open their parcels and enjoy the wonderful aroma. Suggest that they garnish their portions with basil and serve with new potatoes.

serves 4 | *prep* 15 minutes, plus 30 minutes' standing | *cook* 40 minutes

SOLE FLORENTINE

600 ml/1 pint milk
2 strips of lemon rind
2 fresh tarragon sprigs
1 fresh bay leaf
1/2 onion, sliced
50 g/1³/₄ oz butter, plus extra
  for greasing
50 g/1³/₄ oz plain flour
2 tsp mustard powder
25 g/1 oz freshly grated Parmesan
  cheese
300 ml/10 fl oz double cream
pinch of freshly grated nutmeg
450 g/1 lb spinach leaves
4 Dover sole quarter-cut fillets (two
  from each side of the fish), about
  750 g/1 lb 10 oz in total
salt and pepper

TO SERVE
crisp green salad
crusty bread

Preheat the oven to 200°C/400°F/Gas Mark 6. Put the milk, lemon rind, tarragon, bay leaf and onion in a saucepan over a medium heat and bring slowly to the boil. Remove from the heat and set aside for 30 minutes for the flavours to infuse.

Melt the butter in a separate saucepan over a medium heat and stir in the flour and mustard powder until smooth. Strain the infused milk, discarding the lemon, herbs and onion. Gradually beat the milk into the butter and flour until smooth. Bring slowly to the boil, stirring constantly, until thickened. Simmer gently for 2 minutes. Remove from the heat and stir in the cheese, cream, nutmeg and salt and pepper to taste. Cover the surface of the sauce with baking paper or clingfilm. Set aside.

Lightly grease a large baking dish. Bring a large saucepan of salted water to the boil, add the spinach and blanch for 30 seconds. Drain and refresh under cold running water. Drain again and pat dry with kitchen paper. Put the spinach in a layer in the base of the prepared dish.

Wash and dry the fish fillets. Season to taste with salt and pepper and roll up. Arrange on top of the spinach and pour over the cheese sauce. Bake in the preheated oven for 35 minutes until bubbling and golden. Serve immediately with a green salad and crusty bread.

serves 4 | *prep* 5 minutes | *cook* 12 minutes

SOLE MEUNIERE

225 ml/8 fl oz milk
115 g/4 oz plain flour
700 g/1 lb 9 oz Dover sole fillets
25 g/1 oz butter
1–2 tbsp sunflower oil
2 tbsp chopped fresh parsley
salt and pepper
lemon wedges, to garnish

Pour the milk into a large, shallow dish. Spread the flour out on a large, flat plate and season to taste with salt and pepper.

Dip the sole in the milk and then in the flour, turning to coat. Shake off any excess.

Melt the butter with the oil in a large, heavy-based frying pan over a low heat, add the fish fillets and cook in batches for 2–3 minutes on each side until lightly browned. Keep each batch warm in a low oven while you cook the remaining fish. Sprinkle with the parsley and serve immediately, garnished with lemon wedges.

serves 4–5 | prep 10 minutes, plus 10 minutes' soaking | cook 15–20 minutes

WHOLE FRIED FISH
WITH SOY & GINGER

6 dried Chinese mushrooms
3 tbsp rice vinegar
2 tbsp soft light brown sugar
3 tbsp dark soy sauce
7.5-cm/3-inch piece fresh root ginger,
   finely chopped
4 spring onions, sliced diagonally
2 tsp cornflour
2 tbsp lime juice
1 sea bass, cleaned and scaled,
   about 1 kg/2 lb 4 oz
4 tbsp plain flour
sunflower oil, for frying
salt and pepper
1 radish, sliced but left whole,
   to garnish

TO SERVE
shredded Chinese leaves
radish slices

Soak the dried mushrooms in hot water in a bowl for about 10 minutes, then drain well, reserving 100 ml/ 3½ fl oz of the liquid. Cut into thin slices.

Mix the reserved mushroom liquid with the vinegar, sugar and soy sauce. Put in a saucepan with the mushrooms and bring to the boil. Reduce the heat and simmer for 3–4 minutes.

Add the ginger and spring onions and simmer for 1 minute. Blend the cornflour and lime juice together, stir into the saucepan and cook, stirring constantly, for 1–2 minutes until the sauce thickens and clears. Set aside.

Season the fish to taste inside and out with salt and pepper, then dust lightly with flour, carefully shaking off any excess.

Heat 2.5 cm/1 inch of oil in a wide, heavy-based saucepan to 180–190°C/350–375°F, or until a cube of bread browns in 30 seconds. Carefully lower the fish into the oil and fry on one side for 3–4 minutes until golden. Use 2 metal spatulas or fish slices to turn the fish carefully and fry on the other side for a further 3–4 minutes until golden brown.

Remove the fish, draining off the excess oil, and put on a serving plate. Reheat the sauce until boiling, then spoon it over the fish. Serve immediately, surrounded by shredded Chinese leaves and sliced radishes, garnished with a sliced whole radish.

serves 4 | prep 5 minutes | cook 10–15 minutes

SKATE IN BLACK BUTTER SAUCE

4 skate wings, about 175 g/6 oz each
600 ml/1 pint fish stock
225 ml/8 fl oz dry white wine
55 g/2 oz butter
2 tbsp lemon juice
2 tsp capers in brine, rinsed
2 tbsp chopped fresh parsley
salt and pepper

Put the fish in a large, heavy-based frying pan or flameproof casserole, pour in the stock and wine and season to taste with salt and pepper. Bring to the boil, then reduce the heat and simmer for 10–15 minutes until the fish is tender.

Meanwhile, melt the butter in a large, heavy-based frying pan over a very low heat and cook until it turns brown but not black. Stir in the lemon juice, capers and parsley and heat for a further 1–2 minutes.

Transfer the skate wings to warmed serving plates with a fish slice, pour the black butter sauce over and serve immediately.

serves 4 | *prep* 10 minutes | *cook* 10 minutes

HAKE IN WHITE WINE

about 2 tbsp plain flour
4 hake fillets, about 140 g/5 oz each
4 tbsp extra virgin olive oil
125 ml/4 fl oz dry white wine, such
   as a white Rioja
2 large garlic cloves, very finely
   chopped
6 spring onions, finely sliced
25 g/1 oz fresh parsley, very finely
   chopped
salt and pepper

Preheat the oven to 230°C/450°F/Gas Mark 8. Spread the flour out on a large, flat plate and season well with salt and pepper. Dredge the skin side of the hake fillets in the seasoned flour, then shake off any excess. Set aside.

Heat a shallow, flameproof casserole over a high heat until you can feel the heat rising. Add the oil and heat until a cube of bread sizzles in 30 seconds. Add the hake fillets, skin-side down, and cook for 3 minutes until the skin is golden brown.

Turn the fish over and season to taste with salt and pepper. Pour in the wine and add the garlic, spring onions and parsley. Transfer the casserole to the preheated oven and bake, uncovered, for 5 minutes, or until the flesh flakes easily. Serve the fish straight from the casserole.

serves 4 | *prep* 10 minutes | *cook* 10 minutes

GRILLED RED SNAPPER WITH GARLIC

2 tbsp lemon juice
4 tbsp olive oil, plus extra for oiling
4 red snapper or mullet, cleaned
and scaled
2 tbsp chopped fresh herbs, such as
oregano, marjoram, flat-leaf parsley
or thyme
salt and pepper

TO GARNISH
2 garlic cloves, finely chopped
2 tbsp chopped fresh flat-leaf parsley
lemon wedges

Preheat the grill to high. Put the lemon juice, oil and salt and pepper to taste in a bowl and whisk together. Brush the mixture inside and on both sides of the fish and sprinkle over the herb of your choice. Transfer to an oiled grill rack.

Cook the fish under the grill, basting frequently and turning once, for 10 minutes, or until golden brown.

Meanwhile, mix the garlic and parsley together. Sprinkle over the top of the cooked fish and serve hot or cold, garnished with lemon wedges.

serves 6 | *prep* 15 minutes | *cook* 50 minutes–1 hour

FISHERMAN'S PIE

900 g/2 lb white fish fillets, such as
   plaice, skinned
150 ml/5 fl oz dry white wine
1 tbsp chopped fresh parsley,
   tarragon or dill
100 g/3½ oz butter, plus extra
   for greasing
175 g/6 oz small mushrooms, sliced
175 g/6 oz cooked peeled prawns
40 g/1½ oz plain flour
125 ml/4 fl oz double cream
900 g/2 lb floury potatoes, such as
   King Edward, Maris Piper or Desirée,
   peeled and cut into chunks
salt and pepper

Preheat the oven to 180°C/350°F/Gas Mark 4.
Grease a 1.7-litre/3-pint baking dish.

Fold the fish fillets in half and put in the dish.
Season well with salt and pepper, pour over the
wine and scatter over the parsley.

Cover with foil and bake in the preheated oven for
15 minutes until the fish starts to flake. Strain off the
liquid and reserve for the sauce. Increase the oven
temperature to 220°C/425°F/Gas Mark 7.

Melt 15 g/½ oz of the butter in a frying pan over a
medium heat, add the mushrooms and cook, stirring
frequently, for 5 minutes. Spoon over the fish.
Scatter over the prawns.

Heat 55 g/2 oz of the remaining butter in a
saucepan and stir in the flour. Cook for 3–4 minutes
without browning, stirring constantly. Remove from
the heat and gradually add the reserved cooking
liquid, stirring well after each addition.

Return to the heat and slowly bring to the boil,
stirring constantly, until thickened. Add the cream
and season to taste with salt and pepper. Pour over
the fish in the dish and smooth over the surface.

Bring a large saucepan of salted water to the boil,
add the potatoes and cook for 15–20 minutes. Drain
well and mash with a potato masher until smooth.
Season to taste with salt and pepper and add the
remaining butter, stirring until melted.

Pile or pipe the potato onto the fish and sauce
and bake for 10–15 minutes until golden brown.

serves 4 | *prep* 15 minutes, plus 30 minutes' marinating | *cook* 15 minutes

SICILIAN TUNA

4 tuna steaks, about 140 g/5 oz each
2 fennel bulbs, thickly sliced
   lengthways
2 red onions, sliced
2 tbsp extra virgin olive oil
crusty rolls, to serve

MARINADE
125 ml/4 fl oz extra virgin olive oil
4 garlic cloves, finely chopped
4 fresh red chillies, deseeded and
   finely chopped
juice and finely grated rind of
   2 lemons
4 tbsp finely chopped fresh
   flat-leaf parsley
salt and pepper

Whisk all the marinade ingredients together in a small bowl. Put the tuna steaks in a large, shallow dish and spoon over 4 tablespoons of the marinade, turning until well coated. Cover and leave to marinate in the refrigerator for 30 minutes. Reserve the remaining marinade.

Heat a ridged griddle pan over a high heat. Put the fennel and onions in a separate bowl, add the oil and toss well to coat. Add to the griddle pan and cook for 5 minutes on each side until just beginning to colour. Transfer to 4 warmed serving plates, drizzle with the reserved marinade and keep warm.

Add the tuna steaks to the griddle pan and cook, turning once, for 4–5 minutes until firm to the touch but still moist inside. Transfer the tuna to the serving plates and serve immediately with crusty rolls.

serves 4 | *prep* 15 minutes | *cook* 40 minutes

SWORDFISH WITH OLIVES & CAPERS

2 tbsp plain flour
4 swordfish steaks, about 225 g/
   8 oz each
100 ml/3½ fl oz olive oil
2 garlic cloves, halved
1 onion, chopped
4 canned anchovy fillets, drained
   and chopped
4 tomatoes, peeled, deseeded
   and chopped
12 green olives, stoned and sliced
1 tbsp capers, rinsed
salt and pepper
fresh rosemary sprigs, to garnish

Spread the flour out on a large, flat plate and season to taste with salt and pepper. Coat the fish in the seasoned flour, then shake off any excess.

Heat the oil in a large, heavy-based frying pan over a low heat, add the garlic and cook, stirring frequently, for 2–3 minutes until golden but not brown. Remove with a slotted spoon and discard.

Add the swordfish steaks to the oil and cook over a medium heat for 4 minutes on each side until cooked through and golden brown. Remove with a slotted spoon and set aside.

Add the onion and anchovies to the pan and cook, mashing the anchovies with a wooden spoon, until they have turned to a purée and the onion is golden. Add the tomatoes and cook over a low heat, stirring occasionally, for 20 minutes, or until the mixture has thickened.

Stir in the olives and capers and taste and adjust the seasoning, if necessary. Return the fish steaks to the pan and heat through gently. Serve garnished with rosemary sprigs.

serves 2 | *prep* 5 minutes | *cook* 15–20 minutes

TROUT WITH ALMONDS

40 g/1½ oz plain flour
2 trout, cleaned, about 350 g/
   12 oz each
55 g/2 oz butter
25 g/1 oz flaked almonds
2 tbsp dry white wine
salt and pepper

Spread the flour out on a large, flat plate and season to taste with salt and pepper. Coat the trout in the seasoned flour, then shake off the excess.

Melt half the butter in a large, heavy-based frying pan over a medium heat, add the trout and cook for 6–7 minutes on each side until tender and cooked through. Transfer to warmed plates with a fish slice, cover and keep warm.

Melt the remaining butter in the frying pan, add the almonds and cook, stirring frequently, for 2 minutes, or until golden brown. Add the wine, bring to the boil and boil for 1 minute. Spoon the almonds and sauce over the trout and serve immediately.

serves 4 | prep 15 minutes, plus 30 minutes' marinating | cook 25–30 minutes

TROUT IN LEMON & RED WINE SAUCE

Rinse the fish inside and out under cold running water and pat dry with kitchen paper. Put in a single layer in a non-metallic dish. Pour the vinegar into a small saucepan and bring to the boil, then pour over the fish. Cover and set aside to marinate for 30 minutes.

Pour the wine and water into a saucepan and add the bay leaves, thyme sprigs, parsley sprigs, lemon rind, shallots, carrot, peppercorns and cloves and salt to taste. Bring to the boil over a medium–low heat.

Meanwhile, drain the trout and discard the marinade. Put the fish in a single layer in a large frying pan and strain the wine mixture over them. Cover and simmer over a low heat for 15 minutes until cooked through and tender. There is no need to turn them.

Transfer the trout to individual serving plates with a fish slice and keep warm. Return the cooking liquid to the boil and cook until reduced by about three-quarters. Gradually beat in the butter, a little at a time, until fully incorporated. Stir in the chopped parsley and dill and taste and adjust the seasoning, if necessary. Pour the sauce over the fish, garnish with parsley sprigs and serve immediately.

4 trout, cleaned and heads removed
225 ml/8 fl oz red wine vinegar
300 ml/10 fl oz red wine
150 ml/5 fl oz water
2 bay leaves
4 fresh thyme sprigs
4 fresh flat-leaf parsley sprigs,
  plus extra to garnish
thinly pared rind of 1 lemon
3 shallots, thinly sliced
1 carrot, thinly sliced
12 black peppercorns
8 cloves
85 g/3 oz unsalted butter, diced
1 tbsp chopped fresh flat-leaf parsley
1 tbsp chopped fresh dill
salt and pepper

serves 6–8 | *prep 25 minutes* | *cook 35 minutes*

PAELLA

2 pinches of saffron threads
4 tbsp hot water
400 g/14 oz Spanish short-grain rice
16 live mussels
about 6 tbsp olive oil
6–8 unboned chicken thighs, excess
  fat removed, skin on
140 g/5 oz chorizo sausage,
  cut into 5-mm/1/4-inch slices,
  casings removed
2 large onions, chopped
4 large garlic cloves, crushed
1 tsp mild or hot Spanish paprika,
  or to taste
100 g/3 1/2 oz French beans, chopped
100 g/3 1/2 oz frozen peas
1.2 litres/2 pints fish, chicken or
  vegetable stock
16 raw prawns, peeled and deveined
2 red peppers, grilled, peeled
  and sliced
35 g/1 1/4 oz fresh parsley, finely
  chopped
salt and pepper

Put the saffron threads in a small bowl, add the hot water and set aside. Put the rice in a sieve and rinse until the water runs clear. Set aside. Clean the mussels by scrubbing or scraping the shells and pulling out any beards that are attached to them. Discard any with broken shells or any that refuse to close when tapped. Put the mussels into a colander and rinse well under cold running water.

Heat half the oil in a 30-cm/12-inch paella pan or flameproof casserole over a medium–high heat, add the chicken, skin-side down, and cook for 5 minutes, or until golden and crispy. Transfer to a bowl. Add the chorizo and cook, turning frequently, for 1 minute until it starts to crisp. Add to the chicken.

Heat the remaining oil in the paella pan, add the onions and cook, stirring frequently, for 2 minutes. Add the garlic and paprika and cook for 3 minutes until the onions are softened but not browned.

Add the drained rice, beans and peas to the paella pan and stir until coated in oil. Return the chicken and chorizo and any accumulated juices to the pan. Stir in the stock, saffron liquid and salt and pepper to taste and bring to the boil, stirring. Reduce the heat to low and simmer, without stirring, for 15 minutes, or until the rice is almost tender and most of the liquid is absorbed.

Arrange the mussels, prawns and pepper strips on top, cover the pan and continue simmering, without stirring, for 5 minutes, or until the prawns turn pink and the mussels open.

Discard any mussels that remain closed. Taste and adjust the seasoning, if necessary. Sprinkle with chopped parsley and serve immediately.

serves 4 | *prep* 15 minutes, plus 15–20 minutes' soaking | *cook* 45 minutes

STUFFED SQUID

8 sun-dried tomatoes
8 small prepared squid (bodies about
   13 cm/5 inches long)
85 g/3 oz fresh white breadcrumbs
2 tbsp capers, rinsed and
   finely chopped
2 tbsp chopped fresh flat-leaf parsley
1 egg white
olive oil, for brushing and drizzling
3 tbsp dry white wine
salt and pepper
lemon juice, for drizzling (optional)

Preheat the oven to 160°C/325°F/Gas Mark 3.
Put the sun-dried tomatoes in a heatproof bowl
and cover with boiling water. Set aside for
15–20 minutes.

Meanwhile, finely chop the squid tentacles
and put in a separate bowl. Add the
breadcrumbs, capers and parsley.

Thoroughly drain the tomatoes and pat dry
with kitchen paper. Finely chop and add to the
breadcrumb mixture. Mix thoroughly and
season to taste with salt and pepper. Stir
in the egg white.

Spoon the breadcrumb mixture into the squid
body sacs, pushing it down well. Do not fill
them more than about three-quarters full or
they will burst during cooking. Secure the
opening of each sac with a cocktail stick so
that the stuffing will not ooze out.

Generously brush oil over an ovenproof dish
large enough to hold the squid snugly in a
single layer. Put the squid in the dish and pour
in the wine. Cover with foil and bake in the
preheated oven, turning and basting
occasionally, for 45 minutes, or until tender.

Remove from the oven and set aside to cool
to room temperature. To serve, remove and
discard the cocktail sticks and slice the squid
into rounds. Arrange on warmed individual
plates and drizzle with a little oil and either
the cooled cooking juices or lemon juice.

8

Barbecued or griddled, this is the surefire way of cooking fish to enjoy all its natural flavour at its best. In the case of barbecuing, it's also an entertainment in itself, and with all the joys of eating alfresco that go with it. But the griddle offers an excellent alternative if the weather does not measure up to the occasion.

BARBECUES
AND GRIDDLES

Whole fish sizzling on the barbecue is a feast for the eye, nose and ear in advance of the taste buds. You just need to decide on your preferred flavourings – chillies, ginger and lime in Indonesian Spiced Fish, garlic and parsley in Stuffed Sardines or try Bacon-wrapped Trout. Kebabs are also enduringly appealing, and here they feature monkfish and mushrooms, prawns and peppers and scallops and sweetcorn.

serves 4 | *prep* 15 minutes | *cook* 20–30 minutes

HERRINGS WITH ORANGE TARRAGON STUFFING

1 orange
4 spring onions
50 g/1¾ oz fresh wholemeal
   breadcrumbs
1 tbsp chopped fresh tarragon, plus
   extra sprigs to garnish
4 herrings, cleaned and scaled
salt and pepper
green salad, to serve

TO GARNISH
2 oranges
1 tbsp light brown sugar
1 tbsp olive oil, plus extra for oiling

Preheat the barbecue. Then start by making the stuffing. Grate the rind from half the orange using a zester. Peel and chop all the orange flesh on a plate in order to catch all the juice.

Mix the orange flesh, juice, rind, spring onions, breadcrumbs and chopped tarragon together in a bowl. Season to taste with salt and pepper.

Divide the stuffing into 4 equal portions and use it to fill the body cavities of the fish.

Put each fish onto a square of lightly oiled foil and wrap the foil around the fish so that it is completely enclosed. Cook the fish over hot coals for 20–30 minutes until cooked through – the flesh should be white and firm to the touch.

Meanwhile, make the garnish. Peel and thickly slice the 2 oranges and sprinkle over the sugar. Just before the fish is cooked, drizzle the oil over the orange slices, add to the barbecue and cook for 5 minutes.

Transfer the fish to serving plates and garnish with the barbecued orange slices and tarragon sprigs. Serve with a green salad.

serves 4 | *prep* 10 minutes, plus 2 hours' marinating | *cook* 10 minutes

SALMON TERIYAKI

4 salmon fillets, about 175 g/6 oz each

SAUCE
1 tbsp cornflour
125 ml/4 fl oz dark soy sauce
4 tbsp mirin or medium-dry sherry
2 tbsp rice or cider vinegar
2 tbsp runny honey

TO SERVE
1/2 cucumber
mixed salad leaves, torn into pieces
4 spring onions, thinly sliced
   diagonally

Rinse the salmon fillets under cold running water, pat dry with kitchen paper and put in a large, shallow, non-metallic dish. To make the sauce, mix the cornflour and soy sauce together in a jug until a smooth paste forms, then stir in the remaining ingredients. Pour three-quarters of the sauce over the salmon, turning to coat. Cover with clingfilm and leave to marinate in the refrigerator for 2 hours.

Preheat the barbecue. Cut the cucumber into batons, then arrange the salad leaves, cucumber and spring onions on 4 serving plates. Pour the remaining sauce into a saucepan and set over the barbecue to warm through.

Remove the salmon fillets with a slotted spoon and reserve the marinade. Cook the salmon over medium hot coals, brushing frequently with the reserved marinade, for 3–4 minutes on each side. Transfer the salmon fillets to the prepared serving plates and pour the warmed sauce over them. Serve immediately.

serves 4 | *prep* 5 minutes, plus 2 hours' marinating | *cook* 20 minutes

BARBECUED SALMON

4 salmon steaks, about 200 g/
   7 oz each
lemon wedges, to garnish
crisp green salad leaves, to serve

MARINADE
100 ml/3¹/₂ fl oz vegetable oil
100 ml/3¹/₂ fl oz dry white wine
1 tbsp black treacle
1 tbsp brown sugar
1 tbsp soy sauce
1 garlic clove, chopped
pinch of ground mixed spice
salt and pepper

Put the oil, wine, treacle, sugar, soy sauce, garlic and mixed spice in a large bowl and mix until well combined. Season to taste with salt and pepper.

Rinse the salmon steaks under cold running water and pat dry with kitchen paper. Add the salmon to the wine mixture and turn until well coated. Cover with clingfilm and leave to marinate in the refrigerator for at least 2 hours or overnight.

Preheat the barbecue. Remove the salmon steaks with a slotted spoon and reserve the marinade. Cook over hot coals, turning frequently and basting with the reserved marinade, for 10 minutes on each side, or until cooked through. About halfway through the cooking time, add the lemon wedges and cook for 4–5 minutes, turning once. Arrange the salmon on a bed of green salad leaves, garnish with the lemon wedges and serve.

serves 4 | *prep* 5 minutes | *cook* 10 minutes

NUT-CRUSTED HALIBUT

3 tbsp butter, melted
750 g/1 lb 10 oz halibut fillet
55 g/2 oz pistachio nuts, shelled
  and very finely chopped

Brush the melted butter over the halibut fillet.

Spread the nuts out on a large, flat plate. Roll the fish in the nuts, pressing down gently.

Preheat the griddle over a medium heat. Cook the halibut, turning once, for 10 minutes, or until firm but tender – the exact cooking time will depend on the thickness of the fillet.

Remove the fish and any loose pistachio pieces from the heat and transfer to a large, warmed serving platter. Serve immediately.

serves 4 | *prep* 10 minutes | *cook* 6–10 minutes

COD & TOMATO PARCELS

4 cod steaks, about 175 g/6 oz each
2 tsp extra virgin olive oil
4 tomatoes, peeled and chopped
25 g/1 oz fresh basil leaves, torn into
   small pieces
4 tbsp white wine
salt and pepper

Preheat the barbecue. Rinse the cod steaks under cold running water and pat dry with kitchen paper. Using a sharp knife, cut out and discard the central bones. Cut 4 rectangles of double-thickness foil, each measuring about 33 x 20 cm/13 x 8 inches. Brush with the oil. Put a cod steak in the centre of each piece of foil.

Mix the tomatoes, basil and wine together in a bowl and season to taste with salt and pepper. Divide the tomato mixture equally between the fish and spoon on top. Bring up the sides of the foil and fold over securely.

Cook the cod parcels over hot coals for 3–5 minutes on each side. Transfer to 4 large serving plates and serve immediately in the parcels.

serves 4 | *prep* 10 minutes | *cook* 6–8 minutes

BLACKENED FISH

1 tsp black peppercorns
1 tsp fennel seeds
1 tsp cayenne pepper
1 tsp dried oregano
1 tsp dried thyme
3 garlic cloves, finely chopped
2 tbsp polenta
4 monkfish fillets, about
   175 g/6 oz each, skinned
3 tbsp corn oil

TO GARNISH
thinly pared strips of lime rind
lime halves

Crush the peppercorns lightly in a mortar with a pestle. Mix the crushed peppercorns, fennel seeds, cayenne pepper, oregano, thyme, garlic and polenta together in a shallow dish.

Put the monkfish, 1 fillet at a time, in the spice mixture and press gently to coat all over, then shake off any excess.

Heat the oil in a large, heavy-based frying pan over a medium heat. Add the monkfish and cook for 3–4 minutes on each side until tender and cooked through. Serve garnished with lime rind strips and lime halves.

serves 6 | *prep* 15 minutes | *cook* 20 minutes

CARIBBEAN SEA BASS

1 sea bass, cleaned and scaled, about
  1.5 kg/3 lb 5 oz
1–2 tsp olive oil
1 tsp saffron powder
½ lemon, sliced, plus extra to garnish
1 lime, sliced, plus extra to garnish
1 bunch of fresh thyme
salt and pepper

Preheat the barbecue. Rinse the sea bass inside and out under cold running water and pat dry with kitchen paper. Using a sharp knife, make a series of shallow diagonal slashes along each side of the fish. Brush each slash with a little of the oil, then sprinkle over the saffron powder.

Brush a large fish basket with oil and put the fish in the basket, but do not close it. Season the cavity of the fish to taste with salt and pepper. Put the lemon and lime slices and the thyme in the cavity without overfilling it.

Close the basket and cook the fish over medium hot coals for 10 minutes on each side. Carefully transfer to a large serving plate, garnish with lemon and lime slices and serve immediately.

serves 4 | *prep* 15 minutes, plus 1 hour's marinating | *cook* 10–15 minutes

MONKFISH KEBABS

750 g/1 lb 10 oz monkfish,
  skinned and boned
8 button mushrooms
1 red onion, cut into 8 pieces
1 red or green pepper, deseeded and
  cut into 8 pieces
2 courgettes, cut into 8 thick slices
4 tomatoes, halved, to garnish

MARINADE
50 ml/2 fl oz vegetable oil,
  plus extra for basting
1 tsp paprika

Cut the monkfish into bite-sized cubes. Put in a non-metallic dish, pour over the oil and sprinkle with paprika. Mix well. Cover the dish with clingfilm and leave to marinate in the refrigerator for at least 1 hour.

Remove the monkfish from the refrigerator and return to room temperature. Select skewers that will fit on your griddle. Soak wooden skewers in water for 30 minutes before using to prevent burning. Preheat the griddle over a medium heat.

Thread the monkfish cubes onto the skewers, alternating with the mushrooms and vegetable pieces. Put the kebabs on the griddle and cook, turning frequently and basting occasionally with oil, for 10–15 minutes, or until the fish is firm and the vegetables tender. If you wish, place the tomato halves on the griddle for the last 2–3 minutes.

Serve the kebabs on individual serving plates, garnished with the tomato.

serves 4 | *prep* 15 minutes | *cook* 15 minutes

SPICY JOHN DORY

2 John Dory, filleted
2 garlic cloves, chopped
2 shallots, grated
1 small fresh red chilli, deseeded
  and chopped
1 tbsp lemon juice
lemon wedges, to garnish

AIOLI
4 large garlic cloves, finely chopped
2 small egg yolks
225 ml/8 fl oz extra virgin olive oil
2 tbsp lemon juice
1 tbsp Dijon mustard
1 tbsp chopped fresh tarragon
salt and pepper

TO SERVE
crisp green salad leaves
raw and lightly blanched vegetables

To make the aïoli, put the garlic and egg yolks in a blender or food processor and process until well blended. With the motor running, slowly pour in the oil through the feed tube until a thick mayonnaise forms. Add the lemon juice, mustard, tarragon and salt and pepper to taste and process until smooth. Transfer to a non-metallic bowl, cover with clingfilm and refrigerate until ready to serve.

Preheat the barbecue. Rinse the fish under cold running water and pat dry with kitchen paper. Mix the garlic, shallots, chilli and lemon juice together in a separate bowl. Rub the mixture onto both sides of the fillets.

Cook the fish over hot coals for 15 minutes, or until cooked through, turning once. Arrange the fish on a bed of green salad leaves, garnish with lemon wedges and serve, with the aïoli and the vegetables for dipping served separately.

serves 6 | *prep* 15 minutes, plus 1 hour's marinating | *cook* 16 minutes

INDONESIAN SPICED FISH

1–2 sea bream or red snapper, about
  1 kg/2 lb 4 oz
4 garlic cloves, finely chopped
2 fresh red chillies, deseeded and
  finely chopped
2.5-cm/1-inch piece fresh root ginger,
  thinly sliced
4 spring onions, chopped
juice of 1 lime
2 tbsp corn oil, plus extra for brushing
salt
shredded coconut, to garnish
  (optional)

Clean the fish, then remove the scales, beginning at the tail and working towards the head. Rinse the fish inside and out under cold running water and pat dry with kitchen paper. Using a sharp knife, make a series of diagonal slashes on both sides of the fish. Put in a large, shallow, non-metallic dish.

Put the garlic, chillies, ginger and spring onions in a food processor and process to a paste. Transfer to a small bowl, stir in the lime juice and oil and season to taste with salt. Put 1–2 tablespoons of the spice mixture into the cavity of the fish and spoon the remainder over the fish, turning to coat. Cover with clingfilm and leave to marinate in the refrigerator for up to 1 hour.

Preheat the barbecue. Lightly brush a fish basket with oil and put the fish in the basket. Reserve the marinade. Cook the fish over medium-hot coals, basting frequently with the reserved marinade, for 8 minutes on each side, or until the flesh flakes easily. Serve immediately, garnished with coconut, if desired.

serves 4 | *prep* 10 minutes, plus 30 minutes' marinating | *cook* 10 minutes

TUNA & TARRAGON SKEWERS

300 g/10½ oz fresh tuna steaks
450 g/1 lb button mushrooms
chopped fresh tarragon, to garnish

MARINADE
2 tbsp white wine
3 tbsp balsamic vinegar
1 tbsp extra virgin olive oil
1 garlic clove, finely chopped
salt and pepper

TO SERVE
freshly cooked rice
mixed salad

If using wooden skewers, soak them in water for 30 minutes before using to prevent burning. Meanwhile, to make the marinade, put the wine, vinegar, olive oil and garlic in a large bowl, season with salt and pepper to taste, and mix until well combined.

Rinse the tuna steaks under cold running water and pat dry with kitchen paper. Cut into small cubes. Thread the tuna cubes onto the skewers, alternating with the mushrooms. When the skewers are full (leave a small space at either end), transfer them to the bowl and turn in the marinade until well coated. Cover with clingfilm and leave to marinate in the refrigerator for at least 30 minutes.

Preheat the barbecue. Remove the skewers from the marinade and reserve the marinade. Cook the skewers over hot coals, turning frequently and basting with the reserved marinade, for 10 minutes, or until the tuna is cooked through (but do not overcook). Arrange the skewers on a bed of rice, garnish with chopped tarragon and serve with a mixed salad.

serves 4 | *prep* 5 minutes, plus 1½ hours' marinating | *cook* 8 minutes

BARBECUED SWORDFISH

4 swordfish steaks, about
   150 g/5½ oz each
salt and pepper
lime slices, to garnish

MARINADE
3 tbsp rice wine or sherry
3 tbsp chilli oil
2 garlic cloves, finely chopped
juice of 1 lime
1 tbsp chopped fresh coriander,
   plus extra to garnish

TO SERVE
freshly cooked jacket potatoes
barbecued corn on the cob
selection of fresh salad leaves

To make the marinade, put the rice wine, oil, garlic, lime juice and coriander in a bowl and mix until well combined.

Rinse the fish fillets under cold running water and pat dry with kitchen paper. Arrange the fish in a shallow, non-metallic dish. Season to taste with salt and pepper, then pour over the marinade. Turn the fish in the marinade until well coated. Cover with clingfilm and leave to marinate in the refrigerator for 1½ hours.

Preheat the barbecue. Remove the fish with a slotted spoon and reserve the marinade. Cook the fish over hot coals for 4 minutes. Turn the fish over, brush with the reserved marinade and cook on the other side for a further 4 minutes, or until cooked through.

Remove from the heat and garnish with chopped coriander and lime slices. Serve with hot jacket potatoes, barbecued corn on the cob and a selection of salad leaves.

serves 6 | *prep* 20 minutes, plus 1 hour's marinating | *cook* 6–8 minutes

STUFFED SARDINES

15 g/¹/₂ oz fresh parsley,
  finely chopped
4 garlic cloves, finely chopped
12 fresh sardines, cleaned
3 tbsp lemon juice
85 g/3 oz plain flour
1 tsp ground cumin
salt and pepper
olive oil, for brushing

Put the parsley and garlic in a bowl and mix together. Rinse the fish inside and out under cold running water and pat dry with kitchen paper. Spoon the herb mixture into the cavities of the fish and pat the remainder all over the outside of the fish. Sprinkle the sardines with lemon juice and transfer to a large, shallow, non-metallic dish. Cover with clingfilm and leave to marinate in the refrigerator for 1 hour.

Preheat the barbecue. Mix the flour and cumin together in a bowl, then season to taste with salt and pepper. Spread out the seasoned flour on a large, flat plate and gently roll the sardines in the seasoned flour to coat, then shake off any excess.

Brush the sardines with oil and cook over medium-hot coals for 3–4 minutes on each side. Serve immediately.

serves 4 | *prep* 15 minutes | *cook* 10–16 minutes

BACON-WRAPPED TROUT

4 trout, cleaned
4 rindless smoked streaky bacon
  rashers
4 tbsp plain flour
2 tbsp olive oil
2 tbsp lemon juice
salt and pepper
lamb's lettuce, to serve

TO GARNISH
fresh parsley sprigs
lemon wedges

Preheat the barbecue. Rinse the trout inside and out under cold running water and pat dry with kitchen paper. Stretch the bacon using the back of a heavy, flat-bladed knife.

Spread the flour out on a large, flat plate and season to taste with salt and pepper. Gently roll each trout in the seasoned flour until well coated, then shake off any excess. Beginning just below the head, wrap a bacon rasher in a spiral along the length of each fish.

Brush the trout with oil and cook over medium hot coals for 5–8 minutes on each side. Transfer to 4 large serving plates and drizzle with the lemon juice. Garnish with parsley sprigs and lemon wedges and serve with lamb's lettuce.

serves 4 | *prep* 10 minutes, plus 30 minutes' marinating | *cook* 10 minutes

FENNEL-BASTED TROUT FILLETS

4 trout, cleaned and filleted
lemon wedges, to garnish

MARINADE
4 tsp vegetable oil
juice of ¹/₂ lemon
4 fresh fennel sprigs, finely chopped,
  plus extra sprigs to garnish
salt and pepper

To make the marinade, combine the oil and lemon juice in a small bowl and whisk together. Stir in the chopped fennel and salt and pepper to taste.

Put the trout fillets in a shallow, non-metallic dish. Pour over the fennel mixture, cover the dish with clingfilm and leave to marinate in the refrigerator for 30 minutes.

Remove the trout from the refrigerator and return to room temperature. Preheat the griddle over a medium heat. Transfer the trout to the griddle and brush the marinade over the fish. Cook the fillets for 5 minutes on each side, turning once and brushing with the remaining marinade.

Remove the trout from the griddle and arrange on a serving dish. Garnish with fennel sprigs and lemon wedges and serve immediately.

serves 4 | *prep* 10 minutes, plus 1 hour's marinating | *cook* 10–15 minutes

WHOLE GRILLED FISH

4 tbsp chopped fresh mint
4 tbsp chopped fresh parsley
4 tbsp chopped fresh tarragon
4 trout, herring or bass, cleaned and
    scaled, about 350 g/12 oz each
juice of 1 lemon
1 tbsp oil or butter, for brushing
4 tbsp butter, diced
salt and pepper

TO SERVE
freshly boiled new potatoes
French beans with almonds

Mix the herbs together in a small bowl. Put one-quarter of the mixture in the cavity of each fish, reserving a small amount for serving. Gently press the fish closed.

Make 2–3 shallow cuts on each side of the fish. Put the fish in a non-metallic dish. Sprinkle with salt and pepper to taste and half the lemon juice. Rub in well. Cover the dish with clingfilm and leave to marinate in the refrigerator for 1 hour.

Preheat the griddle over a medium heat. Spray or brush with oil.

Dot the fish with half the diced butter, then put, buttered-side down, on the griddle. Cook for 6 minutes, or until the bottom is brown and crispy, then sprinkle the remaining lemon juice on top, dot with the remaining butter and turn over to cook the second side.

Transfer the cooked fish to individual plates and serve with boiled new potatoes and French beans with almonds.

serves 4 | *prep* 15 minutes, plus 3–4 hours' marinating | *cook* 4–5 minutes

PRAWN & MIXED PEPPER KEBABS

24 large raw prawns, peeled and
    deveined but with tails left intact
1 red pepper and 1 green pepper,
    deseeded and cut into small chunks
lime wedges, to garnish
freshly cooked rice or Chinese leaves,
    to serve

MARINADE
2 spring onions, chopped
2 garlic cloves, finely chopped
1 fresh green chilli and 1 small fresh
    red chilli, deseeded and finely
    chopped
1 tbsp grated fresh root ginger
1 tbsp snipped fresh chives
4 tbsp lime juice
1 tbsp finely grated lime rind
2 tbsp chilli oil
salt and pepper

Put the spring onions, garlic, chillies, ginger, chives, lime juice and rind, oil and salt and pepper to taste in a food processor and process until smooth. Transfer to a non-metallic bowl.

Thread the prawns onto skewers, alternating with the red and green pepper chunks. When the skewers are full (leave a small space at either end), transfer to the bowl and turn in the marinade until well coated. Cover with clingfilm and leave to marinate in the refrigerator for 3–4 hours.

Preheat the barbecue. Remove the kebabs from the marinade and reserve the marinade. Cook the kebabs over hot coals, turning frequently and basting with the reserved marinade, for 4–5 minutes, or until the prawns are cooked through (but do not overcook). Arrange the skewers on a bed of rice or Chinese leaves, garnish with lime wedges and serve.

serves 4 | *prep* 5 minutes | *cook* 10–15 minutes

SEAFOOD BROCHETTES

4 live scallops, shucked and cleaned
4 baby squid, cleaned
4 raw tiger prawns, in their shells
4 button mushrooms
4 cherry tomatoes
4 baby sweetcorn (optional)
2 tbsp vegetable oil, for basting
few flat-leaf parsley sprigs, to garnish
buttered rice, to serve

Select skewers that will fit on your griddle. If using wooden skewers, soak them in water for 30 minutes before using to prevent burning. Preheat the griddle over a medium heat.

Meanwhile, thread several pieces of all 3 types of seafood and the vegetables alternately onto each skewer.

Put the kebabs on the griddle and cook, turning frequently and basting occasionally with oil, for 5–10 minutes, or until the fish is firm and the vegetables are tender. Be careful not to overcook the squid, or it will be tough.

Remove the kebabs from the griddle and transfer to individual serving plates. Garnish with parsley and serve with buttered rice.

INDEX